AUTHOR'S NOTE

NAMES and identifying characteristics of certain beautiful people in this book have been changed. Conversations presented in dialogue form have been re-created from my memory of them, but they are not intended to represent word-for-word documentation; rather they are meant to evoke the gist of what was actually said.

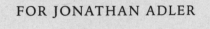

FOR JONATHAN ADLER

ACKNOWLEDGEMENTS

MASSIVE amounts of gratitude to the gorgeous folk and glamorous varmints who enhanced my text by jogging my highly selective memory: I refer to my dad, Terry Doonan; my sister, Shelagh Doonan; my old chum Biddie Biddlecombe (also a sister of sorts); all the Adlers; and, last but not least, my therapist Dr John Pappas.

A *vente* thank you to all the glamorous, recklessly encouraging varmints over at Simon & Schuster, especially my editor, Amanda Murray. Thanks also to: my assistant, Danny Evans; my agent, Tanya McKinnon; my lawyer, James Addams; and my nanny, Marita.

Across the pond, thanks to the beautiful people at HarperCollins including, but not limited to, Sarah Bailey, Claire Kingston, Fiona Marsh and Elizabeth Woabank. Thanks also to Jon Plowman, Caryn Mandebach, Jonathan Harvey and Gary Ventimiglia for believing in the groovy telegenic nelly potential of this book.

Lastly, thanks to my brain for showing me the ugly truth about the Beautiful People.

CONTENTS

INTRODUCTION 1

Chapter 1 **TARTS** 5

Chapter 2 **FUN** 29

Chapter 3 **BLEACH** 39

Chapter 4 **NUTS** 59

Chapter 5 **EYEBALLS** 73

Chapter 6 **CAMP** 87

Chapter 7 **GUTS** 99

Chapter 8 **GIFTS** 115

Chapter 9 **VERMIN** 143

Chapter 10 **DAUGHTERS!** 165

Chapter 11 **PUDDING** 177

Chapter 12 **NO KNICKERS** 199

CONTENTS

Chapter 13   **PUNKS**   217

Chapter 14   **MY WILLIE**   231

Chapter 15   **HOLLYWOOD**   251

Chapter 16   **CREVICE NOZZLES**   271

Chapter 17   **BLANCHE**   279

POSTSCRIPT   295

Some of it wasn't very nice,
but most of it was beautiful.

Dorothy Gale, *The Wizard of Oz*

INTRODUCTION

My MOTHER was a beautiful person. When I was six years old, she sneezed and her dentures flew out. They hit the kitchen floor with a sharp *clack!* and then rattled sideways across the linoleum floor like a fleeing crustacean. I have absolutely no recollection of graduation day, or my 21st birthday, or what I did last Christmas, but as long as I live, I will never forget the sight of glam Betty Doonan in her tight skirt and white stilettos chasing her fugitive dentures.

Am I strange? Quite possibly.

I was born in 1952, the same year that Queen Elizabeth II ascended to the throne. In 2002, fifty years later, Queen Elizabeth and I both celebrated our golden jubilees. Naturally, we both took strolls down our respective memory lanes. While hers was doubtless strewn with ermine capes, bejewelled accessories, sparkling crystal toasting goblets, and well-fed corgis, mine was not.

As I wandered through the windmills and filing cabinets of my mind, I was taken aback by what I found, and did not find.

Yes, there were flying dentures, but where was the more picturesque stuff, the Hawaiian sunsets, the Easter bunnies, and the fluffy kittens? Where were those dreamy summer afternoons spent chasing butterflies through fields of daisies while riding a white Victorian bicycle? Was I too sloshed to recall them? Did they ever exist? And where, most importantly of all, were the Beautiful People?

As a fashion-obsessed, nelly teen growing up in Reading, it was inevitable that I should develop a deranged fixation with the phenomenon known as the Beautiful People. In the 1960s the Beautiful People, or BPs as we devotees called them, were big news. Every fashion magazine was crammed with fascinating drivel about these self-indulgent glamour pusses. No detail of their lives was too trivial for my consideration: I simply had to know everything about their hairdressers, their palazzos, their caftans (the Beautiful People always seemed to be photographed wearing caftans), their eating habits, or lack thereof, and the unguents they slapped on their gorgeous faces. Where did they live? It wasn't Reading for sure. The Beautiful People were totally Euro-fabulous: it was all about Rome and Gstaad and Saint-Tropez. They had never seen, or smelled, the Huntley & Palmers biscuit factory.

What were the qualifications needed to join the BPs? Were there any membership dues? Nobody seemed to know. It was all very mysterious. There were certain common denominators: most Beautiful People seemed to have loads of spare cash, ramparts of thick hair and fake lashes. Having a closet full of Valentino couture seemed like it might speed up the approval process.

The fact that I was several hundred miles away from the nearest Roman palazzo living in a rooming house with a bunch of batty relatives and miscellaneous lodgers only served to fuel my ardour. I daydreamed only of sloughing off the grotty milieu with which fate had seen fit to endow me and escaping to the fashionable excitement of the big (Emerald) city where the Beautiful People were waiting to welcome me into their bracelet-encrusted arms.

So where were they now? Why, when I took that stroll down memory lane on my fiftieth birthday, could I find no trace of them?

Though devoid of BPs, my memory banks were, I hasten to add, by no means empty. *Au contraire!* As I began to write this memoir, I found that they were teeming with vivid recollections. I found half a century of jarring occurrences, freakish individuals, fashion follies, deranged obsessions, public embarrassments, kamikaze outfits, unsavoury types, varmints and vermin. There were hernias and food poisonings, cringe-making encounters with law enforcement, and stomach-churning regrets. There was no shortage of heart-warming material.

Woven through this tapestry of recollections, like a gaudy strand of hot-pink silk, was my family, immediate and extended, in all its raw majesty: my mother, the feisty 1940s' broad; my troubled and anarchic grandmother Narg;

my blind aunt Phyllis; my bra-burning sister Shelagh; and Biddie, my showbiz-crazed childhood best friend.

Revisiting my *temps perdu* proved both cathartic and entertaining. Sometimes I wept, but more often I chuckled. As you may have already predicted, it was not long before I had my Oz epiphany and figured out that there was indeed 'no place like home'. What happened to the Beautiful People? Like Dorothy's mates, they were there all along. I had simply failed to recognise them.

This memoir is intended to set the record straight and pay a bit of long-overdue homage to the *real* Beautiful People, *my* Beautiful People. It's a toast not just to my family and the glamorous varmints I have known, but to all the tarts and trolls and twinkies and trouts who have thrown on an elegant chapeau, or a ratty wig, and gone in search of glamour and fun.

Here's to us! Long live the Beautiful People!

Chapter 1

TARTS

A T THE AGE of 21 I went in search of the Beautiful People.

I was not alone. Joining me on this earnest and passionate quest was a childhood friend. His name was James Biddlecombe, but everyone called him Biddie.

Looking back I realise that Biddie and I were suffering from a mild but persistent affliction. There was no formal diagnosis and no known cure. Our malaise can best be summed up as follows: we were a couple of low-rent, latter-day Madame Bovarys. Like Flaubert's anti-heroine, we saw glamour and modish excitement in the faraway, and only boredom and dreariness in the here and now. In Reading, our industrial hometown, there was no shortage of dreary here and nows.

We fed our fantasies and illusions by reading endless drivel about the Beautiful People in my mother's glossy magazines. These effortlessly stylish trendsetters owned sprawling palazzos in Rome and ultragroovy pieds-à-terre in Chelsea. They slept in six-foot circular beds covered with black satin sheets and white Persian cats. The Beautiful People were thin and gorgeous, and they had lots and lots and lots of thick hair, and their lives seemed to be about a hundred million times more screechingly fabulous than Biddie's life and mine combined. They did not work much, but they had buckets and buckets of money, which they spent on things like champagne and caftans and trips to Morocco to buy caftans.

Soon they would be spending some of it on us. Soon we would be lolling on their Afghani rugs enjoying goulash and hash brownies, and meeting all their bohemian friends at lavishly decadent soirées thrown in our honour.

'What a gas! Here come Simon and Biddie,' one Beautiful Person would whisper to another.

'Intriguing. Do tell . . .'

'Such a divine couple. New in town. A bit common, but otherwise totally happening. I simply must intro-duce you!'

Biddie and I were not a couple per se. As pre-teens, we had once shown each other our 'bits' down by my father's compost heap, but that's about as far as it went. Our relationship was something else. Something equally intense. Something quite spiritual.

Biddie and I were *sisters*. Our sisterly bond began at about the age of six. We clicked because we shared the same camp sense of humour. We had the same interests and disinterests. Biddie and I hated to play conkers or marbles. We preferred to spend our time doing highly nuanced imitations of our female teachers. Their personal style was our obsession: Miss Stoddard's bloomers, Mrs Milner's bowling-ball breasts, sadistic Miss Bagnold's crisp shantung suits.

As we grew older we became more perverse. We developed a shared fascination for anything tawdry or illegal. This included, but was not limited to, the swarthy bloke down the street from Biddie's block of council flats who, though married, was caught soliciting in the public toilets down by the river. He was arrested and denounced in the local paper. Whenever we saw him in the neighbourhood, we would become all giggly and knowing.

By the age of ten Biddie and I had graduated to national tabloid exposés. When the Christine Keeler scandal broke, we thought we had died and gone to heaven. The daily revelations about reefer smoking, interracial sex, and spanking among the bowler-hatted, pompous politicians, the landed gentry, and their female companions rendered us all of a quiver and steamed up Biddie's National Health spectacles.

It was not long before we began to identify with the two high-priced tarts at the centre of this erotically charged hurricane: Biddie was the cheeky blonde Mandy Rice-Davies and I was the enigmatic brunette Christine Keeler, the girl the *News of the World* dubbed 'The Shameless Slut', the girl who brought down the Conservative Government of England.

Not everyone thought these young ladies were as glamorous and interesting as we did. The majority of our little classmates were forbidden to read or watch anything about Mandy or Christine. Biddie and I were only too happy to fill the gaps in their knowledge. In fact, we used the Profumo Affair to institute a reign of terror. Many of our victims would, after a heavy bombardment of salacious details, hold their chubby little hands over their reddened ears and beg for mercy.

We discovered that if we merely chanted the words 'Christine Keeler! Christine Keeler!' over and over again with increasing ferocity, some children could even be reduced to tears. We were eventually caught and punished for this game by a teacher who could barely disguise her amusement.

This incident only served to strengthen our commitment to Mandy and Christine. We admired their moxie. Though barely 20 years old, they had already done quite well for themselves. They hobnobbed with lords and spent their weekends being pampered in large country houses. They were Beautiful People-ish.

By the time we reached the age of 16 – i.e. old enough to become prostitutes – Biddie and I had morphed into reckless fun seekers. We were an anything-for-kicks double act. If we had been girls, real girls, we might so easily have become the next Mandy and Christine. Biddie was tall and exotic and hilarious. His exhibitionism, comedic timing, not to mention his ability to play female leads, had garnered rave reviews for his all-boys high school drama society.

Though mousier, shorter and more secretive, I was even more likely to become a tart than Biddie, albeit of the straightforward male variety. I was the first male person-age in our hometown, preceding even Biddie, to walk into a ladies' jewellery shop and demand a pierced ear.

'Have you thought about a career?' asked Terry, my dad, one day over Sunday lunch. My parents and our ex-tended family of assorted lodgers and mentally ill relatives all craned their necks in my direction, anxious to hear my thoughtful reply.

'Pass the gravy. I'm moving to Paris,' I began, eliciting a gasp of surprise from my blind aunt Phyllis.

'Eiffel Tower!' ejaculated Narg enigmatically. Narg was my schizophrenic grandmother. I reversed her name from Gran to Narg when I was about six, declaring that it suited her much better, which it did.

'I'm going to sell my body on the Left Bank to existen-tialists and people like that.'

Nobody batted an eyelid. With two certified lunatics in

residence – Narg and my uncle Ken – we all had a very high tolerance for startling pronouncements.

My parents, Terry and Betty, should probably have been more concerned. From an early age, I was excessively focused on obtaining the freedom that comes with having a bit of extra cash in my pocket, and was prepared to do whatever it took to get it. I happily washed dishes at the Mars bar factory canteen in nearby Slough. I also put in time at the local cork and bottle top factory; disgusting fauna – snakes, centipedes, and large, orange, powdery-looking spiders – frequently emerged from the bales of Indian cork and crawled up my arm.

I looked upon this period as a warm-up. Consorting with rich old Parisian men, no matter how wizened or grotesque of habit, could not possibly be any more creepy than this, and would probably be a lot more lucrative.

Instead of becoming a prostitute, I went off to university, courtesy of Her Majesty's Government, leaving Biddie in Reading working at the local department store. Three years later I came back with a mediocre and useless general arts degree and found myself in exactly the same position as Biddie, only he was in Soft Furnishings and I was plonked down in Clocks and Watches.

While Biddie unfurled and scissored his brocades and velveteens, and counselled customers about their Lancelot pelmets and Austrian poufs, I flicked a feather duster over my dreary brass carriage clocks and wind-up travel alarms.

Though this was not what I had in mind for us, it had its advantages. In this dusty, suburban retail milieu, we enjoyed fame and notoriety. We were grand *poissons* in a small pond, especially the flamboyant Biddie, who when customers innocently asked, 'Where can I get felt?' could never resist replying, 'Come round the back, dear, and I'll show you what I've got!'

With his long neck, dangly earring, and madly au courant hennaed Ziggy Stardust toilet-brush coiffure, Biddie was the store's biggest personality, and a dead ringer for Mr Bowie. He was pounced upon more than once and asked for his autograph, even during working hours. The good people of Reading took no issue with the notion that David Bowie – Britain's most exciting pop phenomenon – would have elected to spend his days slicing up chintz in a regional department store.

'Berkshire born and Berkshire bred, strong in the arm and thick in the head,' snorted Biddie derisively after encountering these contemptible examples of small-town naïveté.

Though feeling insanely more glamorous than everyone within a 20 mile radius has its obvious benefits, Biddie and I wanted more. We craved fabulousness, mink bedspreads, Beautiful People and popping champagne corks. Our hopes and dreams were incompatible with the esprit of our gritty, violent hometown.

In a desperate and heroic attempt to unearth a bit of *la dolce vita*, Biddie and I joined Reading's only gay club.

Located in the 'functions room' of a pub called The
Railway Tavern, this fortnightly gathering was aimed at
the local homosexualists, the majority of whom were
shockingly provincial and gin-soaked. *Tragic* is another
adjective that springs uncharitably to mind.

Biddie and I dubbed these men the pre-Wolfendens.
This was our sardonic recognition of the fact that they
were old enough to have experienced gay life prior to the
legal changes resulting from the Wolfenden Report. This
landmark document, overseen by an official called Lord
Wolfenden, led to the 1967 Sexual Offences Act, which
finally made it legal for fun-loving blokes like us to have
consensual sex behind our Austrian poufs.

Despite the fact that many of Reading's pre-
Wolfendens had suffered through, and survived, years of
small-town oppression and police entrapment, Biddie and
I were too inert and glamour-obsessed to afford them any
respect. In fact, we went one step further. We actually
managed to subject them to yet further indignities.

One hot summer evening, shortly after I had returned
from my stint in academia, Biddie and I hit the Railway
Tavern dance floor, hard. We were both anxious to
demonstrate our latest Bowie 'moves'. The very instant
we heard 'Suffragette City' we went completely bonkers,
strutting onto the postage stamp-sized disco floor and
posing in imitation of our god.

We had no way of knowing that disaster was about to strike.

One of the organisers of the evening suddenly vacated his seat in front of the folding card table where he had been extracting the cost of admission from new arrivals. He began to mince his way, with some urgency, towards the men's room, via the dance floor.

' 'ere! I bet you can't do this!' yelled Biddie, executing a very impressive back bend.

Long-torsoed Biddie held this position for a split second and then resurfaced, at great speed. In his teeth he clenched a ten-inch-long cigarette holder containing a bright-pink Sobranie cocktail cigarette.

Suddenly, violently and horribly, the thrusting cigarette holder speared the pre-Wolfenden.

The victim let forth a searing yelp of agony. Biddie's white-hot cigarette had burnt a nasty crater in his white, lacy, nylon shirt. The vile and distinctively toxic odour of melting synthetic fabric quickly pervaded the room. Friends of the victim rushed balletically to his aid, offering soothing words while simultaneously directing reproachful glances at the perpetrator. As the molten nylon adhered to the skin of the victim, the agonised moaning increased slightly.

I was overheard speculating that, because of his astounding gin intake, the victim could not possibly be experiencing any pain. Reproachful glances became piercing stares filled with white-hot loathing.

We were banned forever from The Railway Tavern.

We knew the time had come. The writing was on the wall. The pre-Wolfendens of The Railway Tavern were not ready for our particular brand of hip sophistication, nor would they ever be. It was time for us to inflict ourselves on a bigger and more worthy audience. As we clomped home in our platform shoes, we began to strategise our conquest of the Beautiful People.

How hard could it be? London was less than an hour away. On that very night, while we were assaulting pre-Wolfendens at The Railway Tavern, the Beautiful People of Mayfair and Kensington were indulging their whims and fancies and amusing each other with their clever bon mots and their outré outfits.

On the following day we would take the train to London and find the hippest, grooviest, dreamiest apartment. Soon we would be lolling and lounging among the Beautiful People.

'You naughty boys! Where on Earth have you been hiding yourselves?' they would ask rhetorically as they forked exotic morsels into our salivating, ever-widening mouths.

Two weeks later we packed our belongings and ourselves into Cyril Biddlecombe's tiny automobile.

My memory of that momentous, life-changing, bowel-curdling drive to London is quite vivid.

Despite having driven a jeep across Tunisia during

World War II, Biddie's father was a decidedly iffy driver. As long as I live, I will never forget the furious jiggling occasioned by his atrocious gear changing and declutching. The car convulsed and jolted to a standstill just as every traffic light turned green, adding hours to our trip. It was reminiscent of a violent, drunken, ill-timed sexual encounter.

Hideously hungover and encrusted with smudges of Doreen Biddlecombe's and Betty Doonan's maquillage – snagged, without permission, to add pizzazz and sparkle to our going-away party – Biddie and I sat in the backseat trying to control our mirth and our nausea.

On Biddie's lap sat Happy Harry, a horrid ventriloquist's doll in a blue-striped nylon shirt, matching bright-blue pants, and red bow tie. His colleagues had presented Biddie with this hateful object at our going-away party the night before.

Before we had even reached the outskirts of Reading, Biddie had evolved an evil, high-pitched, nasal voice to deliver Happy Harry's nasty pronouncements.

'I can't hurt you. I'm just a little doll,' he would say, pausing for dramatic effect while we stared at Harry's shiny plastic face and buggy eyes. 'Trouble is, you don't know what I'm thinking . . . do you now?'

Happy Harry's taunting was the last thing I needed.

Unbeknown to Biddie, I was already a basket case of gnawing anxiety. I had a terrible dark secret which I could not bring myself to share with anyone: I was going insane.

I was completely and utterly convinced that I was about to lose my marbles. Any day now a horrible madness would descend upon me, and I would end up having a lobotomy just like Narg. My uncle Ken had gone bonkers in early adulthood. Now it was my turn.

I was also convinced that I had done permanent damage to my brain and psyche by taking LSD. Biddie and I had dropped acid together on a grim, wet Monday. This life-changing, dreadful experience gave me a window into the hellish hallucinations of my close family members and left me convinced that I was doomed to share the same fate. If the genes didn't get me, then an acid flashback would. Adding Happy Harry's demonic exhortations to the mix only exacerbated my fears.

''orrible gray skies,' said Happy Harry. 'Wouldn't want it to rain now, would we?'

Happy Harry was right. We were all anxious to get to London before the rain started. We had valuable unprotected cargo strapped to Cyril's roof rack.

On the top of the car was Biddie's massive, rhubarb-coloured floor pillow. He had purchased it, with a discount, at our place of employ. This supersized, overstuffed decorative accessory gave our pulsating vehicle the appearance of an experimental automobile prototype. Passers-by waved enthusiastically as if they were witnessing the inaugural outing of a new gas-powered car.

Biddie's floor pillow was critical to the success of our mission. We could not conceive of leaving it behind. The

Beautiful People all had floor pillows. We knew they did. We had seen the Beautiful People lolling on their squishy floor pillows in trendy Sunday magazine spreads. Even if a Beautiful Person was photographed sitting on a couch or a tuffet or a pouf, there was invariably a floor pillow in the background. If we had any hope of being accepted by the Beautiful People, we needed that floor pillow. It was a calling card of sorts.

Despite the fact that we were quite common and almost completely devoid of Euro-sophistication, we were sure the Beautiful People, once they had the chance to meet me and Biddie, would love us. They would not care that we often drank so much that we became incoherent and belligerent and threw up. They would get used to the fact that we fell over a lot and bored people to death because we never knew when to stop braying through our *Rocky Horror Picture Show* repertoire.

We knew they would overlook the fact that Jimmy lived in a council flat and that I had spent my summers not in Ibiza but in Belfast with my toothless granddad or toiling at the Mars bar factory.

We would conquer the world of the Beautiful People. It would be a home run.

Looking back, I realise that we were suffering from a unique mixture of high and low self-esteem.

It was raining gently by the time we reached our destination.

A majestic, glass-covered colonnade welcomed us to the front door of our gorgeous five-storey, nineteenth-century home. Doreen and Cyril seemed quite impressed by the *Masterpiece Theatre* façade.

The interior was another story.

Cunning developers had taken this sumptuous Edwardian dwelling and, leaving the exterior architecture intact, turned it into a beehive of one-room apartments, specifically aimed at excitable idiots like us. Our new abode comprised the back half of what had once been the ground-floor dining room. The whole set-up recalled Omar Sharif's town house in *Doctor Zhivago after* all the paupers and peasants had moved in and carved it up into tiny hovels.

Seduced by the magnificent architecture, we had triumphantly snapped up this overpriced little dwelling as if it were the last apartment on Earth. It was the first and only pad we had seen. We could have found more extensive and affordable accommodation in far-flung neighbourhoods like Dollis Hill or Clapham, but we were determined to live in a posh neighbourhood. We wanted to be Beautiful People-adjacent. We were very stupid.

We unloaded Cyril's vehicle into our hovel.

Biddie and I began to cram our trendy clothes into the worm-eaten closet while Doreen and Cyril looked on forlornly.

The floor pillow occupied most of the room.

Doreen disappeared to make a cup of tea in the communal kitchen.

She returned moments later carrying chipped mugs of steaming tea and looking vaguely disgusted. She had found a mushroom growing through the kitchen floor.

We sipped our tea in silence, sitting on the floor pillow. It was slightly damp.

Mr and Mrs Biddlecombe bore expressions of worried incomprehension. Doreen's seemed to say, 'Why would you want to leave the comforts of home for *this*?'

Cyril's was slightly different; his seemed to say, 'Why are two normal, healthy young men living in one room, as if it's wartime?'

The Biddlecombes had no idea what was fuelling our impulse to follow the yellow brick road. They were genteel working-class folk: Cyril filled shelves at Marks & Spencer, and Doreen was the mainstay of the Reading and Caversham Laundry. They lived a life of low expectations and budgerigars and preferred, with the exception of an annual vacation to Butlins or the Costa Brava, to stay close to home.

'Poor luvs,' said Biddie as we waved goodbye to his parents from the threshold of our new life, 'they seriously think we'll be back in a couple of weeks.'

'And then we'll marry – bye-bye! – a couple of local slags,' I said, 'and live happily ever after.'

'We're going to – bye! – take this town by storm!'

'We'll show 'em!'

'Byeeeee!'

No sooner had Cyril and Doreen jiggled and jolted out of sight than the phone jangled auspiciously. The instrument in question was a payphone located conveniently, or so we initially thought, in a smelly cupboard in the hallway, next to our front door.

Enthusiastically assuming the role of receptionist, I leapt to answer it. At the very least it was probably a fabulous new showbiz opportunity for Biddie. I braced myself to assume the role of hard-boiled theatrical manager.

'Can I speak to Miss Ping, top froor preese?' said the heavily accented caller. I slogged my way to the top of the house only to find that Miss Ping was not *chez elle*.

Over the next hour the phone jangled continuously with random calls for the 20 tenants of various nationalities. It wasn't long before we faced the grim reality that none of the calls were for us and started yelling, '*Phone!* Top froor frat!' up the stairwell with fatigued hostility.

The phone turned out to be the least of our problems.

The overpopulated building, especially the plumbing, was on the verge of collapse. Shared bathrooms and kitchens did nothing to alleviate the appalling strain on the ancient pipes. At about three o'clock in the morning, the sinks and toilets and baths all began to yodel and thump and gurgle.

The next morning, our enthusiasm undimmed, we hit the streets in search of employment.

Waving his soft-furnishings credentials, Biddie had no problem securing a position at the famous Heal's home design store on Tottenham Court Road. The beau monde all shopped at Heal's. Biddie anticipated spending his days guffawing and ingratiating himself with oodles of floor pillow-purchasing Beautiful People.

Biddie found to his surprise that there was a major national economic recession under way: even the Beautiful People had tightened their purse strings. The lack of customers meant Biddie's days were spent napping behind the place mat displays, catching up on sleep lost to our rowdy plumbing and hiding from his colleagues.

He described his co-workers as 'posh but brain-dead'. The mostly female staff had all been to fancy schools but no college. They were relentlessly upper class, horsey and incredibly silly. They said very 1920s things like 'Doooo come over for mulled wine and Wensleydale cheese! You can meet Nigel and Clarinda. It will be toooo toooo ripping!'

These gals had never met exotically common people like us who wore women's 1940s Bakelite bracelets, smoked through cigarette holders, and called each other 'stupid cunt' without thinking twice about it. We had curiosity value for these Charlottes and Henriettas, who I might add, did *not* have any floor pillows *chez eux* and were therefore of very little interest to us.

I was having slightly more luck finding the Beautiful People than Biddie.

I took a job dressing windows at Aquascutum, the snottiest raincoat shop on Regent Street. Here I met a hilarious, well-heeled older gentleman who seemed to have the makings of a Beautiful Person. He did not need his pay cheque but chose to while away his days selling trench coats to aristos and Japanese businessmen because it amused him. This petit eccentric was known among the staffers as the Baroness.

The Baroness was so called because of his fancy Belgravia address and his even fancier black-marble-clad basement flat, wherein he entertained regularly.

The Redgraves were neighbours. If you stood on the Baroness's toilet seat, waited for the flush to stop gurgling and angled your head a certain way, you could just about hear them on their back patio trying to outrant each other about left-wing causes and the latest theatrical scandals and triumphs.

Even more excitingly, the Baroness lived a couple of houses down from Lord Lucan, the notorious gambling aristocrat who, only months prior, had bludgeoned his children's nanny to death. He had mistaken her for his wife, the Countess Lucan. When he realised his error, he clobbered the countess as well and left her for dead. With the aid of friends in high places, Lord Lucan then went on the lam and has not been seen since. The Lucan story was the big news of 1975, and the Baroness basked in the reflected tabloid glare. Biddie and I were only too happy to bask in the reflected glare of the reflected glare.

The Baroness was generous, fun, glamorously situated and, most tellingly, he had loads of floor pillows. Despite all this, we were beginning to suspect that he might not be one of the Beautiful People, especially given his habit, during cocktail parties, of slipping off his caftan and standing stark naked in the ornamental fountain in the middle of the living room, spotlit by one of those colour-wheel revolving lights. Though he was undeniably in good shape and well-tanned from regular trips to Marbella, the Baroness's ornamental years were long gone.

And that light fixture was a bit rusty. It would squeak poignantly while our host stood waiting for a polite round of applause.

No, the Baroness was not one of the Beautiful People. You might say he was Beautiful People-adjacent.

The Baroness notwithstanding, London was hardly the whirligig of fabulousness we had anticipated. It was hardly fabulous at all. Our day-to-day lives were pretty much as turgid as they had been in Reading. We remained, however, insanely optimistic and terminally excitable.

While waiting to be swept into the bracelet-encrusted arms of the Beautiful People, we kept boredom and madness at bay with regular trips to the Malaysian Simulator, an educational installation located perma-nently at the nearby Commonwealth Institute.

The Malaysian Simulator was a dark, gallery-sized room, the walls, ceiling and floor of which consisted of back-projection screens. Visitors to this little-known, free-of-charge multisensory extravaganza consisted of Biddie, myself and the occasional homesick Malaysian.

'You will now be transported to Malaysia,' intoned a
Big Brother voice as we gazed in awe at the entrancing images of rice fields, painted elephants, and beautiful dancing
girls wearing exquisitely applied eyeliner and silver, pagoda
like hats.

'You will now experience the extreme humidity of
Malaysia,' warned the voice as gusts of hot, moist air
rushed into the darkened, magical room via strategically
placed vents and up our fashionably wide trouser bottoms.
We visited the Malaysian Simulator several times a week.
This warm-weather mini-break provided a compelling and
addictive antidote to the grim reality of our new lives, our
rooming house, and our new neighbour Rita.

As previously stated, Biddie and I were paying an
extortionate rent in the hopes of finding ourselves
Beautiful People-adjacent. Instead of the Beautiful People,
God had sent us Rita.

Mopheaded Rita, with her black roots and split ends,
was what Doreen Biddlecombe would have called 'a sorry
sight'. She was a petite, badly preserved, bitter, thirty-
something, exhausted white female. Though she looked
tragically depressed, I can't really comment with any
conviction on her moods or feelings since she was
profoundly unfriendly and showed no interest in becoming chummy with us.

This was really quite stupid of her. Biddie and I worked
well with stylistically challenged females. We would have

taken an enthusiastic interest in tawdry Rita and restyled her hair and found a way to make her feel special.

We would have invited her over for some of Biddie's Findus frozen 'boil-in-the-bag cod in butter sauce'. Scrambling to subsist without Doreen's home cooking, Biddie adopted this dish as his main source of protein. (On one memorable occasion he incurred a small but nasty cod-butter burn on the forehead when one of the aforementioned bags ejaculated unexpectedly. It was his own fault: he was trying to bite it open after being unable to locate a pair of scissors.)

Effortlessly, we would have become Rita's willing confidants, commiserating with her about the impenetrable psyches and uncouth, stinky ways of the male gender, a subject with which we, as fresh-faced twinkies, were just beginning to grapple.

After some hot, greasy cod and girly chit-chat, we would have dressed Rita in groovy vintage crêpe dresses stolen from jumble sales and then dragged her off for a promenade down Portobello Road. We would have told her with relentless conviction how amazing she looked.

Rita needed us. Her personal style was a disaster. With her white plastic footwear – slingback stilettos or shiny vinyl boots – and her red patent plastic mini-trench, she was not only tacky but astoundingly unfashionable. We marvelled at the archetypal sleaziness of her look. Clearly, she had no idea what a floor pillow was. She was not one of the Beautiful People. She was one of the unsavoury people.

Every evening Rita would sally forth in her démodé finery with an air of what can only be described as the very opposite of perky optimism. As we watched our monosyllabic neighbor lurching off into the drizzle, we wondered if she would come back in one piece.

She did.

Like a battered old homing pigeon, Rita somehow always managed to find her way back to her roost, and, because of the intimacy of our living conditions, we were always acutely aware of her return.

The noise was specific and distinct: it was the noise of an inebriated prostitute trying repeatedly and unsuccessfully to insert her key in her own front door. This scratchy, irritating cantata went on for about five minutes and was accompanied by Rita repeating the phrase 'Sod it!' and, if there was a man in tow, making all kinds of depressing double entendres about not being able to 'get it in the hole' etc.

If we were feeling philanthropic, we would put her out of her misery and open up the front door, for which service we received no thanks from grumpy Rita. Kicking the front door closed with the thick heel of her white boot, Rita would then stagger towards her own apartment door, where the key-insertion shenanigans would begin anew.

This interminable racket was, however, only a warm-up. Once inside her abode, Rita took centre stage and the real performance began: throat clearing, the unzipping of boots, smokes and coughs, slaps and tickles, unapologetic belching, and the sound of someone peeing in her own sink (we did that too) were all clearly audible.

After some desultory grumbling and mumbling, usually about money, the copulating would start. There is no way to describe the horrifying, apocalyptic Wagnerian symphony of noises that would erupt once our neighbour began to service her clients. Suffice it to say, it was loud, and the thin skin of Masonite that separated our two abodes, rather than acting as a sound barrier, merely amplified the erotic activities of our white-boot-loving neighbour.

Maybe she was really enjoying it, or maybe she was just hell-bent on making her clients feel like they were performing well, or maybe she was screaming at the agony of her life. Whatever the case, this was the one arena in which Rita allowed herself to be operatically expressive.

'Sounds like someone's fucking her with a floor lamp,' remarked Biddie in his Happy Harry voice, after we had once more been roused from slumber by Rita's primal howling and wailing.

More often than not, the plumbing would get in on the act, banging and screaming and gurgling along with Rita. There was no way that we, even if we were completely drunk, could ever sleep through this auditory onslaught.

Corpselike from exhaustion, we lay side by side under our respective stained and threadbare candlewick bedspreads, silently praying that the cacophony would subside at some point before daybreak.

Thanks to the telepathy that comes from long-standing friendships, I knew we were both having the same thought. Maybe Doreen and Cyril were right. Maybe we should have stayed in Reading at our safe suburban department store, where the motto was 'Never knowingly undersold' and nobody knew what it meant and everyone thought we were special. The smiling faces of the good people in Soft Furnishings and Clocks and Watches wafted through my sleep-deprived consciousness, beckoning me back to Reading and a simpler, more wholesome life.

Rita's screeching finally subsides.

The sodium street lights flood our domestic squalour, silhouetting the floor pillow, making it look a bit like Ayers Rock, and casting a pall on our demented quest. On top of the wardrobe sits Happy Harry, who by now has come to personify my impending madness.

Will we ever find the Beautiful People? Will I go stark raving bonkers in the Malaysian Simulator? Stay tuned.

Chapter 2

FUN

POVERTY is vastly underrated.

In the 1950s, my parents were broke. Despite the lack of cash, Betty and Terry remained glamorous. When their favourite shoes wore thin, they inserted slivers of cardboard into the soles and continued to wear them.

During most of this decade, my family and I lived on the top floor of a dilapidated rooming house in Reading. Ours was a two-room flat with no kitchen or bathroom. Betty, wearing spike heels, carried our water up the stairs in buckets. This did wonders for her already shapely legs.

Terry, who also had good legs, was unemployed at the time. While Betty pounded the streets scrounging clerical jobs, Terry whiled away the hours teaching himself Latin. His goal was to gain entry to the University of Reading, where Latin was an annoying and archaic requirement. It was during this period of leisure that my dad became our personal couturier, hand-sewing little outfits for me and my sister, Shelagh.

Terry was exceptionally versatile. His skills extended way beyond dead languages and sewing. During this rooming-house period, he also designed and constructed most of our furniture. He scrounged orange crates from the local greengrocer and transformed them into chicly minimal *occasional* tables. They really were *occasional,* in the very strictest sense of the word. Most of the time they were orange crates, but occasionally they were tables.

Terry's skill diversity was equalled by the diversity in his own personality: sometimes he was very butch and sometimes he was quite fey. More often than not, he was both. He was the kind of bloke who could repair his own motorbike while listening to Maria Callas on the radio and weeping. He loved women, but he was never *one of the guys*. With his taste for ascots and opera and Latin, he was the ideal parent for an emerging invert such as myself.

Betty and Terry always referred to this cardboard-in-shoe period as the happiest time of their lives. Why? It was a combination of things: they were young and in love; they were proud to have helped kill Hitler; and they were happy to have escaped their respective families. They had yet to encumber themselves with any strange lodgers or mentally ill relatives.

Terry successfully taught himself Latin but was still unable to gain entry to university. He abandoned his academic aspirations and took a position working night shifts in the BBC news department. His job was to monitor Radio Moscow and keep the world apprised of any Cold War developments.

During the day, instead of sewing and sawing, he now slept.

Life, for my sister and me, now took a Dickensian turn.

Shelagh and I were sent to the orphanage.

There was no such thing as day care in Reading in the 1950s. Ever resourceful, my parents went to the local orphanage and made an arrangement to drop us off every day. Cunningly they referred to it as 'the Nursery'. Either way, it was a grim, underfunded, state-run institution.

The orphanage kids were not only violent and unpredictable but also prone to diarrhoea and vomiting and dreadful, streaming colds.

My sister is still furious about the orphanage years. She bridles with outrage when she recalls Johnny, a boy who repeatedly stole, and wore, her red Mary Janes. Johnny's other favourite trick was to pile us both into a perambulator and push us over a precipice.

The orphanage was very *Lord of the Flies*. We even had our own Piggy, a Down's syndrome child called Roderick.

It wasn't long before my sister and I joined the unsupervised mob of evil toddlers who persecuted poor Roderick on a daily basis. Shelagh was complicit in a dreadful game where Roderick was run over repeatedly by a tricycle. Recalling the drama and cruelty of our orphanage years can reduce the good-hearted Shelagh to tears in about thirty seconds.

I am definitely less scarred by this period than my sister. Though the orphanage years left me terminally prissy and germ-phobic, I like to think we were somehow privileged. Not everyone gets to hang out with rage-filled, love-starved orphans at such an early age. We were given a perspective on life that is not afforded to every child. At the orphanage we came face to face with the hoodlums and grifters and headline makers of tomorrow.

Saturday was our day to recuperate from the miseries of the orphanage. While Terry slept, Betty racked her brains to think of ways to keep us entertained. With limited resources, the pressure was on. Ere long, our mother had figured out a winning and very unusual formula: she developed a knack for turning mundane events into whirlwinds of hysterical excitement. Under her supervision, the opening of a soup can became the most insanely thrilling movie premiere on Earth.

'Who wants to watch me put on my bracelet???!!!'

'Someone in the room is going to paint her nails!! Who is it??!!'

'Gather round. There's a bus coming up the hill. You don't want to miss it!!!'

We soon got the hang of it. Betty was the MC and we were the salivating audience. We understood our role. On cue, and at the drop of a hat, our job was to become totally apoplectic and frenzied.

'Who wants to play with an envelope?'

'Yeeeeeeeeeeeee!'

'Stop screaming! You'll wake up your father!'

In no time we had learned to scream silently.

One rainy Saturday there was a lull in Betty's fun factory. She seemed to have run out of ideas. Panic-stricken, she scampered downstairs to the shared kitchen. She returned seconds later carrying the battered tin that contained our favourite food: miniature chocolate Swiss rolls. Extracting one small log, she proceeded to cut it into minute slices. She then arranged them enticingly on a bright-pink plate. With a bold flourish, she placed her offering on one of Terry's occasional tables. Without further ado, Betty tore my teddy bear from my arms.

'Today is . . . *Teddy's birthday!*' she hissed, in a stage whisper which raged with pent-up excitement. My sister and I pogoed up and down appreciatively and as quietly as possible.

From this day forth, Teddy's birthday became the ultimate panacea.

It's freezing and there's no heat and we all have double pneumonia – *it's Teddy's birthday!!*

It's been raining all weekend and we can't go outside because we've all got cardboard in our shoes – *it's Teddy's birthday!!*

Teddy's head fell off – *it's Teddy's birthday!!*

Teddy's birthday never seemed to lose its sizzle. There was no limit to the number of days in a row we could celebrate this occasion with the required levels of verve and hysteria.

One Saturday, Betty had an epiphany, or possibly an attack of cabin fever. Or maybe she had finally OD'd on Teddy's birthday.

'It's time you kids saw the World!' she announced, grabbing her handbag and throwing on her favourite garment, a white, flared mohair steamer coat with three-quarter-length sleeves.

Betty's new concept was inventive, bold, yet incredibly simple. We would go to the local bus station and take a round-trip ride to a neighbouring town in the Thames Valley. Which town? Any town. What could be simpler? What could be more fun? The scenery was not much to look at, but with Betty's unstoppable showbiz enthusiasm, how could it fail to be anything other than grippingly scintillating?

And yet it wasn't.

It was completely and utterly horrible.

Confined in our seats, all we could do was stare out of the window. And at what? England, merry England, whizzing by in all its rain-soaked wretchedness. The vista was both boring and incredibly sad. Not even Betty, with her glass-half-full, manic optimism, could put a spin on the montage of monochromic misery that confronted us. It is forever etched in my memory.

So many appalling tableaux spring to mind! I distinctly remember seeing a middle-aged woman in plastic rain hat standing on a street corner looking as if she were about to burst into tears. Nearby a young mother, probably unmarried, is pushing a pram through dog poop while cursing at her mewling brat. I remember a group of little boys staring at something horrible squashed on the pavement, and groups of little girls trekking across a bomb site and looking furtively behind them as if a beast of some description were following them.

'What the hell is wrong with these bloody English people?' said Belfast-born Betty, who lost no opportunity to contrast the joie de vivre of the Irish with the unmitigated dreariness of the English.

Betty pointed out a red-faced man in Tyrolean hat. We all perked up a bit. Then we saw that he was sitting next to a homeless senior citizen who was cooling her gums with an ice lolly shaped like a rocket.

England, merry England.

The bus stopped every now and then. On one occasion, a bunch of unruly kids piled on. I recognised them from the orphanage. They stood on the seats with their muddy feet and screamed at each other.

'Why can't we do that?' I asked sincerely.

'Because we are different,' replied Betty with queenly emphasis.

The bus continued its journey through Kafka country. The view was dominated by factories, smokestacks, and municipal buildings. There were no rosy-cheeked milk-maids or herds of brown cows with silky lashes.

The soot-blackened industrial sprawl was depressing enough, but worse still were the residential areas where the citizens of England lived out their short, untwinkly lives.

The streets were so small that, even from the vantage point of our bus, we could see comfortably into the living rooms and bedrooms of the passing houses. I observed a worn-out, prematurely aged mother scrubbing the steps of her tension-racked terraced house. Inside a man was swatting large flies on his window with a rolled-up newspaper. Upstairs a demure lady wearing a twinset and pearls clutched a letter which obviously contained bad news.

Next door a lonely secretary was eating beans on toast at six o'clock, illuminated by the cold, grey flickering light of her telly. She will finish her food by 6.20pm, and then what? How about an evening stroll down by the gasworks?

The 1950s were grim. Nobody is to blame. That's just the way it was.

In this rushing panorama of English life, recreational activities appeared to be extremely limited: taking a constitutional next to a polluted canal; dozing in a bus shelter; briskly walking to the local butcher's shop.

Housewives emerged from these establishments clutching bloody packages containing lamb chops or miscellaneous offal. They looked vaguely disgusted, as if they had been sold rotten meat. If anyone in England ever celebrated Teddy's birthday, we certainly never witnessed it.

The bus stopped again. A very tall, severe woman with a crew cut climbed aboard. She was wearing a shirt and tie, a tailored army greatcoat, and flat men's wingtip shoes. We recognised her. She was the receptionist at the local doctor's office. Her name was Fern, and she sometimes wore a monocle.

Betty smiled.

Fern acknowledged Betty, saluting in a military fashion.

It was Rhett Butler doffing his chapeau to Scarlett O'Hara.

Fern's air of masculine chivalry immediately restored order to the bus. The orphanage kids stopped spitting and wiping their phlegm on one another. Everybody onboard made slight postural adjustments. Fern had that effect on people.

Fern took her seat across the aisle. Betty and Fern caught each other's eyes again and quickly looked away.

They had something in common.

They were two self-invented people wordlessly acknowledging one another.

On the next hill, the engine stalled. The bus stopped. The bus went quiet. We hoped it would not roll back down the hill and into the canal. Fern projected an aura

of reassuring competence. We waited anxiously for the
deafening engine to start again.

My sister broke the silence.

'Why is that lady dressed like a man?' she shrieked at
the top of her lungs. Everyone turned around to look at
Fern. Fern stared straight ahead. Betty lit a cigarette.

Betty glared at Shelagh, but Shelagh did not see. She
was too busy staring at the fabulously androgynous Fern.
Was she seeing the glimmering signposts to her own
lesbian future?

'Well? Why *is* she dress – '

RRRooarrh!

The bus lurched forwards. Betty exhaled a sigh of
relief and nicotine and smoke.

Much to Betty's relief, we were soon back at the bus
station.

It was getting late. Terry would be leaving for work
soon. If we hurried, we could all celebrate Teddy's birthday together.

★

★

★

Chapter 3

BLEACH

'My mother is called Betty, but her real name is Martha. She bleaches her hair and she drinks gin.'

I wrote this mini profile when I was nine years old. It was part of a school essay. Our assignment was to describe each member of our family.

I do not recall how I described the rest of my nearest and dearest. I remember Betty's blurb because, for years to come, she would hold up the incident as an example of my compulsion to focus on the tawdry and unwholesome, to the exclusion of anything more cheery or heartwarming.

'Oh, great! I can hardly wait till parents' night,' said Betty as she pored over the essay, having just poured herself a sizeable gin and tonic.

'What about my weekly pottery class? You could have mentioned the silver cup I won for flower arranging.'

I did not really understand her point. It was not as if I had made the whole thing up. We all knew she bleached her hair. And damn good it looked too! Martha Elizabeth Doonan was, hands down, the most charismatic, glamorous mum in the neighbourhood. She wore white pencil skirts, seamed stockings, maquillage, and figure-accentuating, long-line girdles. Next to Betty, the other kids' teetotal mothers, in their sensible flats and sweater sets, looked like a bunch of middle-aged men dressed up as Queen Elizabeth on one of her off-duty corgi days.

And, yes, she drank gin. Uncle Peter, a family friend, worked for an illustrious London gin company. A bachelor and a bon viveur, he was no stranger to what he called the 'sample room'. As a result, our sideboard was invariably groaning with stolen gin of various genres and vintages. On Friday nights he would ride over to our house on his motor scooter with a bottle of gin strapped insouciantly to the passenger seat.

Gin and bleach aside, it was a shock to me that Betty could not quite grasp the overwhelmingly complimentary thrust of my essay.

Betty Doonan examined her reflection in her compact mirror. She was checking on the status of the complex, much-admired hairdo into which she funnelled so much creativity. With a sigh of resignation, she took the bottle of peroxide out from under the sink.

'I can't imagine what Mrs McCann must think of me,' she said as she began to touch up her roots.

Mrs McCann was not really concerned with the likes of Betty Doonan. Nor were any of our teachers. More's the pity. They could have learned a thing or two from Betty Doonan. Betty was fun. Betty looked great. Betty smelled great. Betty made the world a more glamorous and amusing place. Betty was life-enhancing, and Betty judged everything and everybody on the basis of whether or not they too were life-enhancing.

Our teachers would never have qualified. They were not life-enhancing. They were life-corroding and life-disembowelling. While my home life was all gin and bleach and fun, school was the exact opposite.

To describe our teachers as 'dour' would be inaccurate. They were completely and utterly Stalinist. Every school day was more of a gulag-fest than the last.

There was nothing pedestrian about the way these gals enhanced our lives. They were extremely creative. Whether tying us to chairs with our own skipping ropes or subduing us with terrifying gusts of flatulence and halitosis, our tormentors were full of surprises. And, lucky me, I arrived just as an entire generation of these angry women were ambling into the menopause.

Our day started with morning assembly, which was staged and choreographed with totalitarian flair. Punctually and wordlessly, we filed into the gymnasium in our green and grey uniforms accompanied by Miss Stoddard on the piano.

What cheery, uplifting selections did she favour to start the day? 'All Things Bright and Beautiful'? 'There Are Fairies at the Bottom of My Garden'? Much too prissy. With amazing libidinal passion and skill, Miss Stoddard pounded her way through 'In the Hall of the Mountain King'. Edvard Grieg's ominous, throbbing anthem conjured the hellish kingdom of the Norwegian trolls and their dark and horrible leader, the Mountain King. With her relentless pounding, Miss Stoddard gave our morning gatherings a distinct feeling of impending folkloric genocide. She had brought us together only to eradicate us. We would never have thought of staging any kind of uprising. We were just a bunch of worthless little trolls, and we knew it.

Once assembled, we scabby-kneed trolls were called upon to sing gruesome, unlife-enhancing Anglican hymns about choosing 'the steep and rugged pathway' and not wanting to linger 'by still waters'. There was no mention of gin or bleach. The message was simple: the more grim life is, the more character building will be its effect, especially upon wretched little trolls.

After a couple more hymns, we would repair to our various classrooms. These were designated as either A or

B. It was a simple enough system: at the beginning of each year, the smart trolls were sent to A classes and stupid trolls went to B classes. Smart trolls were being groomed to attend the local grammar school, the gateway to a life of middle-class contentment. B troll boys like me were headed for the secondary modern school and thence to a grim, fiery apprenticeship in sheet-metal welding, which was very troll-like, if you think about it.

Girl trolls fared better. They could look forward to, among other options, a hairdressing apprenticeship. This had a certain appeal to me. I had frequently assisted Betty in the application of her bleaching unguents.

It was around this time, not uncoincidentally, that I started to consider the possibility of gender reassignment.

One night, when Betty was tucking me in, I impulsively told her that I had decided to become a girl.

'My name will be Clare,' I said, assuming a wistful demeanour, 'and I will have very, very long blonde hair.'

Betty smiled enigmatically and stared at the space on the pillow around my head where one day soon that long blonde hair would lie in all its flaxen glory. Turning out the light with a jangle of her heavy bracelet, she advised me not to share my secret with anyone in my little B class or with that nasty Mrs McCann. She might not understand.

Betty was right.

Mrs McCann would never have understood. Mrs McCann had never thought about the possibility of gender reassignment. Mrs McCann did not think about anything much, except Canada.

Mrs McCann had recently returned from Canuck country. She had traversed that continent on the Canadian Pacific Railway. The double-decker observation car had afforded Mrs McCann a spectacular view of the endless wheat fields. For some reason she found this very life-enhancing. In fact, she returned from this trip having fallen hopelessly and madly in love with wheat.

She elected to share her new passion with us, over and over again. In lesson after lesson, Mrs McCann dragged us from one side of Canada to the other, while encouraging us to marvel at the immense, golden nothingness of it all.

Once she got warmed up, Mrs McCann would stride about in front of the blackboard, twitching her dirndl skirt and tossing her dry, crinkly torrent of split ends, which coincidentally had the consistency of wheat.

No detail of her sojourn was too small for our consideration. After the wheat fields, she introduced us trolls to the concept of grain silos and then more grain silos and still more. Time and time again her chalk would break as she passionately scrawled endless statistics on the board relating to the vastness of the Canadian prairie, number and size of silos, and the inconceivably massive amounts of grain that poured forth from 'The World's Breadbasket'.

Her travelogues were supported with brochures and personal snaps: Mrs McCann boarding a train;

Mrs McCann staring into the middle distance on an observation platform; a grain silo; a wheat field; another silo. To this day, I cannot look at a loaf of bread without thinking of Mrs McCann and the holiday of a lifetime which she shared with us over and over again, ad nauseam, ad delirium.

Her thinking was no doubt as follows: 'Since these trolls and trollettes will never ascend to the level of society that permits transcontinental Canadian vacations, let them vicariously enjoy mine.'

It was inconceivable to me that Mrs McCann could find this stuff interesting or glamorous. Statistics about grain silos and wheat fields would never have held the attention of anyone in my house. The gin-fuelled, witty repartee which sizzled and crackled between my parents and their friends was infinitely more titillating and engaging.

And getting more so.

Not only did we have free gin but we now had free wine, gallons and gallons of it.

It all started after we took a mind-expanding trip of our own. It wasn't very far, and it didn't take very long, but when we returned we were changed forever.

One day in the early 1960s, Betty, Terry, my sister Shelagh and I took the train up to London and visited the Ideal Home exhibition.

This sounds like it might have been a gigantic yawn, but nothing could be further from the truth. Here, in booth after booth, we deprived post-war curiosity-seekers encountered something beyond our wildest dreams. Talk about life-enhancing! There were free beverages! Free hors d'oeuvres! Chips and dips! Crackers and nibbly bits! Cheeses of the world, and bizarre things like anchovies, all proffered by attractive, enthusiastic young men in tight trousers.

I was experiencing, at no charge, my very first stand-up finger buffet!

The scene, however, lacked the gentility normally associated with such events. Unself-consciously and ungratefully, we plebs crammed handful after handful of exotic morsels into our mouths without any regard for the provenance thereof. It was more like feeding time at London Zoo.

Eventually we reached satiation point. Stuffed to the gills, we staggered off in the direction of the kitchen appliances, little knowing that our lives were about to change forever.

Nestling in between the chip fryers, cheese cutters, and ice-cream makers, we discovered a whole booth dedicated to amateur winemaking. For some reason my parents seemed a lot more interested in this than in the pasta makers or the Chinese noodle-frying kits, or even the free snacks!

Before you could say 'cirrhosis of the liver', my dad was forking over some cash.

Within days of returning home, Terry Rothschild Lafite Doonan had gone into production.

It's no exaggeration to say that my parents went completely berserk. They filled every single inch of our house with vats and vats of gurgling, fermenting wine; there were jugs and buckets and flagons of it. Every time you opened a cupboard, you were confronted by some aspect of the winemaking process. The stench of yeasty fermentation, along with the sound of drunken laughter, is among the most the abiding memories of my childhood.

Occasionally there were leaks and disasters. A vat of homemade blackcurrant *vin rouge* exploded in the attic right next to blind Aunt Phyllis's room. As it drip, drip, dripped onto Betty through the ceiling of her all-white bedroom, it gave her the distinct impression that Aunt Phyllis had been murdered in the windowless garret in which she slept.

Nobody baulked at the mess or inconvenience. Château Doonan was so fruity and sweet that everyone, all the assorted lodgers and relatives, knocked it back with ever-increasing enthusiasm. We entered an era of bacchanalian largesse during which, between Uncle Peter's gin sample room and Terry's ad hoc winery, no Doonan ever darkened the door of the local liquor store again. It wasn't a hobby, it was a lifestyle, an utterly intoxicating lifestyle.

My dad was beside himself, especially when he found out that you could make wine from just about anything.

'It makes you wonder why they bugger about with grapes in France when you can make a delicious wine from potato peelings,' he guffawed as he secreted yet more bottles of tea-leaf and parsnip wine in the crawl space under the living room floor.

It was not long before Terry figured out that he could magically increase the intoxication level simply by adding more sugar at the right juncture. As a result, Château Doonan became more of a rich, fruity sherry than a wine.

Terry made gallons and gallons and gallons of it, which meant we could then drink gallons and gallons and gallons of it. Which is what we did. By the time I hit my teens, I was sloshing a dollop of Château Doonan in my Ribena, and learning to love the warm, comforting glow that ensued.

Terry's *vin extraordinaire* and Uncle Peter's gin played a very important role in the day-to-day functioning of our family. Simply put, alcohol took the edge off. Alcohol was the low-cost prescription that enabled Betty and Terry to deal with the strains and unpredictability of life with batty Uncle Ken, not to mention the crazed and belligerent Narg.

'*Narg put her bloomers in the oven and set them on fire!*'

Slosh, gurgle, swallow. 'No problem!'

'*Uncle Ken rode his bicycle into the canal!*'

'Bottoms up! Is he okay?'

'*Narg hurled insults at the ladies from the Women's Institute!*'

'Mmmm! Try this! What did she actually say?'

This is not a new concept. Lunatics have always driven their caretakers to drink. Grace Poole, nurse to the mad

Mrs Rochester in Charlotte Brontë's *Jane Eyre,* springs easily to mind: 'an able woman in her line, and very trust-worthy, but for one fault – a fault common to a deal of them nurses and matrons – *she kept a private bottle of gin by her,* and now and then took a drop over much'.

We had two Mrs Rochesters, so we needed twice as much booze.

My mother, I hasten to add, was not a sloppy drunk like Grace Poole. *Au contraire!* Betty Doonan could 'hold' her liquor. Though she drank every day for years, I have never once seen her plastered. Holding one's liquor was a highly prized ability and seemed, in Terry and Betty's milieu, to correlate with strength of character. People who could not hold their liquor were spineless toerags, while people who could hold it were thought to be much more important and valuable to society.

The accolades heaped upon Betty for her drinking abilities were nothing compared to those she received for her hair.

As I reflect upon the complexities and contradictions of Betty's life, and of the 20th century in general, I realise that they both found full expression in that incredible hairdo.

Betty was always a rule breaker. As a child, she kept a pet pig. When the circus came to town, she played truant from school in order to carry buckets of water to the zebras. She befriended the clowns, who cheered loudly as she tore round the sawdust-filled ring on her tricycle.

In her 20s, rebellious Betty flew the coop, joined the Royal Air Force, and changed the direction of her hair. Gone was the dowdy, chin-length bob of her childhood. Instead, she adopted the complex upswept, bulbous hairstyle known as the Force's Roll. This new hairdo had a transformative effect. She was no longer Martha, the small-town girl who left school at 13 to churn butter and butcher pigs at the local grocery store. Martha had been replaced by Betty, the confident, sassy, lipstick-wearing broad with the Eve Arden wit.

The new hairdo was infinitely more flattering and imposing than her previous 1930s bob. Formerly five feet, one inch, Betty now stood tall at five feet, seven inches, thanks to three inches of suede platform and a corresponding measurement of hair. The sculptural pompadour which now rose above her forehead not only added height but offset the impact of her large Roman nose. She now looked less like an American Indian and a lot more MGM. Like Bette Davis in *Now, Voyager,* Betty Gordon had travelled the road from troll to siren simply by reversing the direction of her coiffure. What had previously gone down now went up.

Betty met Terry in a soup kitchen after the war. They married two months later at a register office on a date that neither of them could ever remember, thereby relieving us forever of the obligation to do anything as bourgeois as celebrate their wedding anniversary.

For the next fifty years Betty slept with Terry, and with

a full head of hair rollers. The roller at the nape of her neck would frequently become dislodged during the night and work its way to the middle of her back. As a result Betty often dreamt that Zulus were chasing her and prodding her with their spears.

Her morning toilette in front of the small gas fire in her bedroom always took at least an hour. While we unkempt slobs shovelled our breakfast alongside our lodgers and nutty relatives downstairs, Betty would be upstairs painting and primping and coiffing.

Betty worked at it. She had no illusions. She knew she wasn't Grace Kelly. Rather than long to be something she wasn't, she took pride in her ability to improve on what God had given her. Her philosophy could be summed up as follows: 'Even if you happen to be a Northern Irish peasant, you can still, with the right techniques, learn to make a pleasing and life-enhancing impression. It is your duty not to inflict your innate troll-like appearance upon the people around you and to do everything in your power to camouflage it.'

Becoming a blonde was part of this process. Becoming a blonde was also highly therapeutic. It provided Betty with a continuous outlet for her Irish Protestant temper. The quest for the perfect shade of blonde gave focus to her combative streak. She was a highly visual broad with a naturally sophisticated colour sense who was utterly obsessed with the tone of her hair. She had to have the perfect shade of blonde. This became her Holy Grail.

Her quest took her to see a woman called Madge, whose eponymous hair salon served our neighbourhood. I remember Madge, the salon and the person herself, as if it were yesterday. This cramped, steamy hothouse of femininity reeked of perfume and something called hair lacquer. Before hairspray in aerosol cans, there was hair lacquer, a nasty brown liquid which came in medicinal-looking, opaque plastic, squeezable bottles.

I logged many hours at Maison Madge listening to the wheeze of the lacquer bottles and inhaling the chemical, toffeelike smell of their contents. Betty's hair needed lots of extra lacquer. It had to withstand the rush of wind which jiggled it when she rode home on the back of Terry's motor scooter.

Madge was a woman with a mission. Her concept was to bleach every client's hair ice-blonde and then, on successive weeks, coerce her into trying a novelty colour tint. Madge's employees, who had names like Queenie and Sylvia, all had the same ice-blonde hair. Every week they would try a new pastel colour tint. Queenie would be pink one week and violet the next. Sylvia even went pale green.

Betty had nothing but contempt for this kind of pointless experimentation. 'I don't want to look like a tart!' she would say, fending off Madge and her horrid tints, and unintentionally insulting Queenie and Sylvia.

All Betty wanted was the perfect shade of Grace Kelly blonde. Was that too much to ask?

Time and time again I would hear her complaining to

the lodgers that Madge had 'bollocksed' up her hair yet again. Yet again it had 'come out brassy'.

Brassy-blonde is too warm in tone. It has too much orange. It looks like dark-brown hair that has been dyed blonde, which was what Betty's was. Betty wanted people to believe she was a blonde.

Her quest continued into the 1960s. By now her vintage hairstyle was starting to have curiosity value. My friends at school commented on it, and on her over-painted Joan Crawford lip line.

Madge canvassed Betty to adopt a more current style. Her hair was now officially two decades out of date. Under pressure from Madge and Queenie *et al.* Betty capitulated, but with a caveat: she would change her hair but it must remain up. She would never go down.

Accordingly, Madge scraped her hair back into a cluster of large tunnel curls, which sat on her head in the yarmulke region. This look was augmented with dangly earrings and false eyelashes. One wet Saturday afternoon, Betty strode into the house, yanked off her plastic rain hood, and unveiled her new look. Silence. We were not sure what to say. Betty now looked horribly cheap. Though she was always painted and dressed, Betty was never cheap-looking. Until now. This new tarty, hard-faced, crowlike, unfamiliar Betty got the thumbsdown *chez nous*, even from blind Aunt Phyllis. Betty stuck her head under the kitchen faucet and demolished Madge's handiwork. After pouring herself a comforting glass of elderberry-potato wine (Terry was experimenting with improbable ingredient combos), she began the painstaking task of reconstructing her signature hairdo.

Betty had had it with Madge and her crazy ideas. From then on she did the whole job herself. She purchased all the necessary paraphernalia, including professional scissors and two evil-looking two-inch metal clips. These were worn above the ear whenever she was not in public and guaranteed that the hair at the temple was going in the correct, i.e. upwards, direction. We referred to these as her 'electrodes', as in 'Hey, Mum, you forgot your electrodes!' They became objects of amusement. Schizophrenic Uncle Ken, who lived on the second floor and was a frequent recipient of electric shock treatment, seemed unfazed by this insensitivity. He chuckled along with the rest of us.

In the 1970s there was a massive 1940s retro explosion. Betty's entire look, including platform shoes, came screaming back into fashion. She was frequently accosted by young girls asking her where she got her hair done. Betty was delirious. She contemplated opening her own salon and putting Madge out of business.

Betty cut and styled her own hair for the rest of her life. There was a short break in the 1980s when she broke her shoulder and Terry took over. He did his best but was unable to get the requisite height. 'It's bad enough being in agony without having to look like a bloody washerwoman,' said Betty ungratefully.

Finally, in her 70s Betty eschewed peroxide and allowed her hair to grow out. With her steely grey coiffure, she never looked better. Her entire look – maquillage, coiffure, unlifted face and tailored wardrobe – came gorgeously together. And she knew how good she looked.

It was around this time that Betty began to indulge in a bit of revisionist history. She started to deny ever having been a bottle blonde. At first she claimed that the bleach period had lasted only a few months. Before long she was denying ever having done it.

I called her one day in the late 1990s when she was going through chemotherapy. 'A young lady from social services is coming round today with some wigs,' she cackled malevolently. Betty loved nothing more than to watch a do-gooder fall flat on her face.

I wondered if Betty had made any attempt to forewarn the lady about her Byzantine hairdo. Since Betty's hair was upswept, there would be no way to augment it unless with an expensive custom hairline wig. Pull-on wigs went down. Only hairline wigs went up.

'Have you described your hair?' I asked tentatively.

'No. I thought it would be fun to see what this trout comes up with,' replied my mum, who had no idea that referring to the other females as 'trouts' might ever be considered offensive.

The trout arrived, took one look at Betty's thinning, complex coiffure, handed over a bag of cheap pull-on wigs, and fled. This wig bag provided Betty and Terry with endless amusement. They even staged a fashion shoot, using the horrid wigs, in the backyard of their bungalow and sent me the resulting pictures. Perched on a stool, the formerly glamorous Betty in her pull-on wig looks like a horrid little hobbit. She no longer makes a pleasing and glamorous impression. She voluntarily picked this moment, while staring her mortality in the face, to let down her guard and remind the world what a fabulous job she had done of concealing her inner troll, and of enhancing our lives.

Her impudent expression seems to say, 'If I weren't such a generous and glamorous person, I would have subjected you to *this*! Instead I elected to transform myself, for which gargantuan lifelong effort you should be eternally grateful.'

Betty saw her vanity as a component of good manners. It was life-enhancement for everyone. No charge! According to her, we owed it to each other to make an effort. She did not engage in deranged attempts to turn back the clock. She did not waste money on pointless skin-care unguents or self-punitive procedures. For Betty, beauty was a positive thing, a life-affirming, creative force.

When she was on her deathbed, yet another well-meaning, breezy trout materialised in the hospital room doorway and offered her assistance with what was left of her hair.

By this time pain-racked Betty was venomous and irate. She insisted on smoking in her room and would berate me for trying to substitute low-tar ciggies for her usual brand. She would take one drag, remove the cigarette from her mouth, snap off the filter, and reinsert the offending item in her mouth while giving me a look of withering contempt.

'Let's see what you can do,' challenged Betty, eyeing the fresh trout with a mixture of faux-encouragement and malevolence.

I decided to avoid the inevitable fracas and leave them to it. As I walked down the hallway, I could hear Betty berating and abusing her new friend.

'Not down . . . up . . . up! *Up!*'

Chapter 4

NUTS

THE WHOLE set-up reeked of Narg.

The downstairs hallway was almost completely blocked by a large pile of junk. The placement, though clearly the work of a mad person, was nonetheless strategic. The assorted members of our household were now obliged to Matterhorn over it in order to enter the house, reach the stairs, or access any of the main-floor rooms.

I examined the mound. There was some old-fashioned kitchen paraphernalia: a meat grinder, a rolling pin and a rusty, encrusted potato masher. I also saw furniture: Narg's rocking chair and a broken step stool. Against the wall was a heavily stained ironing board supporting an arrangement of depressing souvenirs in various shapes and sizes: a tea towel from Ulster emblazoned with the famous red hand; a hideous paperweight from Belfast; and a sand-filled glass lighthouse from the Isle of Wight. On the top of the pile was a chocolate box filled with old birthday cards and holiday postcards.

At seven o'clock, Terry roared home from work on his motor scooter. I came downstairs and clambered back over the junk. We – my mother Betty, my aunt Phyllis, my sister and I – sat down to dinner. Narg and Uncle Ken were dining à deux in the adjacent room, which also functioned as Narg's bedroom. We could hear Narg's radio blaring. It seemed louder than usual.

Pleasantries were exchanged. Parsnip wine was uncorked. Even though we had all been obliged to navigate it, nobody mentioned the ominous pile of detritus in the hallway.

Suddenly the door burst open. Narg charged into the room like a stampeding cow. We turned our heads in her direction and continued chewing. We all resembled cows: it was a bovine tableau. Our grazing had been interrupted by the arrival of an angry heifer.

It was clear from Narg's expression that she was not in the best of moods.

'It's time for a few home truths!' she shrieked, surveying the room with wild eyes. There was a pause. We waited. We anticipated. We winced. Then it started. A volley of unrepeatable accusations was lobbed at pretty much everyone in the room, including Aunt Phyllis and her guide dog, Lassie. Eventually Narg ran out of breath and tore out of the room.

This was more than just the typical Narg mood swing. Something was up. Narg had clearly made the transition from deranged but benign in-law to fire-breathing maniac.

Nobody said anything.

'Better get back to work,' said Terry. He stood up, donned the battered tweed sports coat with the leather elbow patches that he wore through my entire childhood, and returned to his night shift, leaving the rest of us barricaded in our living room.

Narg paced the floor of her adjacent room. Narg cranked up the radio.

In a hushed and excited tone, Betty attempted to shed some light on our current predicament. According to Betty, Narg's freak-out had been triggered by an altercation between herself and Narg. The subject of the argument was Hawo the cat. This friendly beast was dubbed Hawo because he always seemed to be saying 'Hello'. Hello became Hawo, because, according to my cat-obsessed mother, he could not pronounce his *l*s.

Hawo had recently become sick with feline influenza – or fewine infwuwenza as he would have called it himself. Betty had asked Narg *not* to let Hawo run outside. Fireside warmth was critical to his recovery. Narg had ignored Betty and left the window open. Hawo escaped. Hawo got sicker.

Betty had dealt with years of circusy unpredictability from her mother-in-law, as had we all. Narg was a classic paranoid schizophrenic, post-lobotomy. She had arrived *chez nous* not long after her operation. The surgery was deemed a success: she no longer believed that Martians were beaming rays into her living room. The hallucinations were gone. What was left was a Vegas blockbuster of disinhibited, antisocial behaviour. Narg could always be relied upon to *tell it like it is.*

I well remember our first Christmas together. I was about six. On Christmas Eve, Narg came to wish me goodnight. Popping her head round my door, she found me wide awake and in a high state of excitement. I was convinced that I had just heard the sound of sleigh bells tinkling in the distance. Since Narg was no stranger to the concept of hearing things, I thought she would be a good person in whom to confide such a piece of information.

'Listen! Can't you hear Santa's sleigh bells?' I asked with a misty-eyed, festive look.

'No, I can't, and neither can you!' said Narg bluntly as she clutched her mauve, rubber hot-water bottle to her ancient bosom with her white-knuckled, blue-veined hands.

'But I'm sure I – '

'There are no sleigh bells, because there is no Santa Claus.'

Beat.

'Merry Christmas!' she shrieked and was gone.

~

Life with Narg was not without its chuckles. My sister and I identified strongly with her love of anarchy. We were almost proud of her: none of our playmates had a wacky relative like Narg. Their grandmothers never paraded boldly down the hallway in their old-fashioned Edwardian bloomers.

Whenever 'God Save the Queen' played on the radio, Narg would stand to attention until the very last note, sending us into fits of giggles. Was she making fun of our monarch? I could never quite tell if her allegiance was a hundred per cent sincere. Knowing Narg, she probably went back and forth.

At the time of the Hawo incident, Narg had been living with us for about six years. Her abrasive unpredictability had long since lost its charm. For Betty, a huge animal lover, the Hawo debacle was the last straw.

That morning, while we were at school, she had taken the unprecedented step of politely reprimanding her psychotic mother-in-law. Betty's admonishing tone had taken Narg utterly by surprise. Having been a card-carrying lunatic for so many years, Narg was completely unused to being criticised or held accountable. She had always enjoyed the carte blanche accorded to mobsters, aristocrats, circus clowns and lunatics.

Narg had not reacted well to being cross-examined. Unable to put her feelings into words, she decided to create an art installation. She dashed into her quarters, grabbed every single thing we had ever given her, and hurled it into the hallway. *Et voilà!* The Matterhorn.

The next few weeks were interesting. Every day we picked our way over Narg's discards. We were terrified to move anything. You never quite knew when Narg was going to spring into action, slamming doors, shrieking reproaches, and venting years of accumulated ire and general insanity. It was not long before she tired of performing before her immediate family. The Reading Town Centre became her stage.

One overcast Saturday, about two weeks after the Hawo incident, I was walking down the local high street with my pal Biddie and his dad, Cyril Biddlecombe. We had just been to see a movie called *The Belles of St. Trinians,* a goofy 1950s comedy – entirely suitable for two camp twelve year olds such as ourselves – about a bunch of recalcitrant, slutty schoolgirls.

As my eyes adjusted to the daylight, I spotted a familiar silhouette on the horizon. It was Narg. She was jackbooting down Reading High Street towards us while staring up at the sky. I ducked in behind Cyril's Pacamac.* Too late! She had spotted me through its semi-transparent plastic murk.

Letting forth a high-pitched scream of maniacal glee, Narg barrelled towards us, arms outstretched, at about 30 miles an hour. Terrified shoppers leapt out of her path.

---

*Pacamac: an unstylish but extremely popular brand of lightweight raincoat made of semi-translucent grey plastic. Umbrellas were thought to be effeminate. Real men wore Pacamacs.

If Narg had been an exotic eccentric who wore peacock feathers and massive wigs and brooches, her behaviour would have seemed far less disturbing. But Narg's personal style lacked any surprises. She was, in fact, profoundly average in every aspect of her appearance. Unlike my mother, who always stood out in a crowd, Narg, with her dour crochet knits, straight skirts, flat shoes and string shopping bag, exuded the same ordinariness and frumpiness as did every other old gal shopping for support hose in Marks & Spencer. There was something hideously and unspeakably terrifying about seeing one of these granny archetypes – i.e. Narg – go totally off her rocker while others of her genre moved discreetly away and tried desperately to avoid eye contact.

Salvation appeared in the form of a double-decker bus. Cyril, Biddie and I alighted and escaped, leaving Narg ranting incoherently on the pavement.

One week later, on a sun-dappled Saturday afternoon, Narg appeared fully dressed at the top of the stairs, suitcase in hand. 'I'm off!' she yelled and began to stomp down the stairs with amazing agility and speed. When she got to the front gate, she turned around and yelled back into the house at nobody in particular. 'Simon will never forget his granny!'

Narg then walked out of our lives forever. She journeyed one block south and took up lodging with a poor unsuspecting lady down the street.

To say Betty and Terry were relieved is an under-
statement. Suffice it to say, there was much guzzling of
Château Doonan potato wine that night.

My joy at Narg's departure was mixed with a lingering
feeling of uneasiness. What exactly had she meant by
'Simon will never forget his granny'? None of us would
ever forget Narg, that much was obvious. So why had she
singled me out? What was she planning? Had she selected
me to join her in the land of the loonies at some unspeci-
fied point in the future?

I felt like a marked man.

My parents' euphoria faded quickly. The following morning they woke up to a potato wine hangover and a jolt of
reality. The burden of Uncle Ken's care – his food, his
laundry and his complex medications – had now
descended onto their shoulders.

(Much as it pains me to compliment the two people
who imported Narg into our home in the first place, I
have to admit that Betty and Terry always embraced the
responsibility of their problematic in-laws without a lot of
whining. If there is a Nobel Prize for taking care of
extremely frightening relatives, I would like to think that
my parents are under consideration.)

Uncle Ken was pleasant, blond and quite good-
looking. Like Narg, he was a paranoid schizophrenic.
Despite their common diagnosis, they were quite different. While Uncle Ken was more generally appealing than

Narg, he was infinitely more out of it. Narg's lobotomy had made her somehow more present.

Uncle Ken had only a glancing connection with reality. He was often to be seen having conversations with invisible people or performing strange pantomimes involving various aspects of the coal-mining process. Kenneth had been a mining engineering student at the time of his departure from his trolley. He was quite nostalgic about his night shifts 'down the pit'.

Now he worked as an attendant at the Arthur Hill Memorial Swimming Baths. My sister and I were frequent visitors to this institution. Ken always seemed pleased to see us. He would acknowledge our presence by dumping large buckets of powdered chlorine onto us while we were swimming. It was nice to get preferential treatment.

Our first ensemble dining experience constitutes my strongest memory of Uncle Ken.

It started off auspiciously enough. Ken seated himself next to me. I was happy. It was like having a big brother.

Then the food arrived.

The minute Ken's plate hit the table, it was as if a starting pistol which only he could hear had been fired. He grabbed his knife and fork and attacked his food, eating noisily and with astonishing speed.

'Slow down, for God's sake! Savour the flavour!' begged Terry of his younger brother, but to no avail.

Gobbling food was probably a habit he picked up in the asylum prior to arriving *chez nous*. Meticulous, refined mastication was doubtless out of the question in such an establishment: there was no shortage of aggressive inmates waiting to swipe your grub off your plate if you did not shovel it down your gullet in record time.

Having wolfed down his lunch in a matter of seconds, Ken retired to a fireside armchair. Here he rolled the first in a long series of handmade cigarettes. He performed this skill without watching his hands. He just stared into the middle distance.

Uncle Ken did not make eye contact easily. He had a strange habit, when addressed, of focusing his gaze on one's upper forehead. If you wanted to look him in the eyes, you were obliged to stand on tiptoes. This worked for only so long. After a while his gaze would ascend once more, obliging one to fetch a stepladder or throw in the towel.

'How was lunch?' said my mum, little knowing that an incomprehensibly dreadful and unforgettably nasty series of events was about to take place. Straining to get into his field of vision, she stood on tiptoes and repeated the question.

'Hello. . . Yes. . . Betty. . . Thanksverymuch,' Ken replied incomprehensibly and raised his gaze.

From my vantage point, everything then seemed to go into slow motion and to cut, cut, cut in a cinematic frenzy. It was all very reminiscent of that scene in *The Birds* when

Tippi Hedren observes the unfolding mayhem from a phone booth. I was Tippi.

Scene one: Uncle Ken takes a long drag on his hand-rolled ciggie and exhales in a wheezy rush. Cut.

Just at that moment, Hawo, the ailing cat, walks into the frame. Cut.

Betty rises from the dining room table and heads towards the kitchen with an armload of dishes, addressing the cat on the way with a 'Hello, Hawo!' Cut.

Close-up on Uncle Ken's feet. Cut.

Soundtrack builds.

Hawo looks at Uncle Ken.

Close-up on dilating cat's pupil.

Hawo walks calmly towards Uncle Ken.

Hawo stares malevolently at Uncle Ken's shoes.

Hawo vomits on Uncle Ken's shoes.

The actual vomiting takes several seconds, but Uncle Ken is too out of it on horse pill tranquillisers to do anything other than stare blankly and continue to enjoy his raggedy home-made cigarette.

Cut to Betty who, oblivious to the unfolding drama, lights a fag, pours herself another glass of Château Doonan, and sets about washing the dishes.

Cut back to Ken. Maybe it's that hastily gobbled lunch, or maybe it's the fact that his feet are now covered in foul-smelling cat vomit, or both, but Uncle Ken starts to go a bit green. He stares at the vomit, and the vomit stares back.

Uncle Ken suddenly stands bolt upright (hand-held camera). He has a wild, confused look about him. He lurches out of the dining room and into the kitchen, towards the sink. He elbows Betty out of the way and vomits into the sink full of dishes.

Holding her fag in her bright-orange-rubber-glove-covered right hand, Betty stares out of the window. It's hard to read her expression. Cigarette ash falls.

'The almond tree needs pruning. The branches are hitting the buses again. Better be getting back to work,' says Terry and departs.

Fade to black.

It was then, after the cat-vomit episode, that I became utterly convinced I would end up just like Ken, doomed to a life of deranged misery. I knew that schizophrenia was hereditary. I had read all about it in one of the moderately glossy current-affairs magazines which came gratis with our Sunday newspapers. Now I could clearly see my future unspooling before me in a grim montage of hallucinations, electric shock treatments and nicotine.

My life was already beginning to unravel, just like one of Ken's horrible-smelling cigarettes. I had failed the entry examination for the grammar school. Even Biddie had managed to get into the bloody grammar school! It was now official: I was an idiot. What was the difference between an idiot and a lunatic? Not a lot.

It was hard to feel bubbly and jazzed about my future.

I would probably stay at the idiot school until I turned 16. After that, if I had not already gone bonkers, I would get a job at the Huntley & Palmers biscuit factory. I would work there until I fell into some heavy machinery or went mad or both.

I would wish away the remainder of my days staring at people's foreheads with nothing to look forward to except the occasional deluge of cat vomit.

Salvation appeared in an unexpected form.

One day, while crawling round the floor of my parents' incredibly untidy bedroom in search of Hawo, I happened upon the very meaning of Life, or so I thought at the time.

Next to my mother's bed I found a copy of a swanky magazine called *Nova*. On the cover was a picture of a ravishingly brittle, glamorous Italian socialite.

'Principessa Pignatelli plucks each hair off her legs with tweezers,' read the cheeky headline. 'With that dedication and £5,348 a year to spare, you too might make ninth on the best-dressed lists.'

I took the magazine to my room. Snuggling excitedly onto my bed, I began to read and reread the intoxicating editorial about Principessa Pignatelli. A vain fashion junkie, Luciana Pignatelli criss-crossed the globe, travelling with a vast wardrobe of Valentino couture, ankle weights and eight or nine hairpieces. She resided in a glamorous, floor-pillow-strewn Roman palazzo. She was one of the Beautiful People.

Oblivious to the viciously sardonic tone of the editorial, I instantly developed an infatuated identification with the jet-setting Luciana. I was particularly impressed by her beauty tips: 'She splashes the insides of her thighs with cold water and never puts her breasts in hot water because it makes them sag.' The regimental order and glamour of her life contrasted sharply with the tawdriness and unpredictability of my own. I became obsessed.

I could not imagine any Uncle Kens daring to vomit into *her* sink while she was doing *her* dishes. If she got up to pee in the night, I was sure nobody leapt into the corridor, as my grandmother Narg frequently did, and accused *her* of being a streetwalker.

She was the anti-Narg and the un-Ken.

On first reading, the principessa's world seemed depressingly remote.

Italy seemed such a long way away. The only place we ever travelled to was strife-torn Belfast to check in on my belligerent grandpa.

As I splashed the insides of my thighs with cold water, I thought about the Beautiful People. I did not care how far away they were, I would find them and befriend them.

And soon, very soon, they would like me enough to pretend that I was one of them.

Chapter 5

EYEBALLS

I ONCE took my blind aunt Phyllis out for a walk and fractured her skull.

She wasn't really my aunt. Phyllis was one of a gaggle of women, friends of Betty and Terry, whom we referred to as *aunt*.

There was Auntie Iris with the tunnel curls, whose attractive Polish husband had lost both legs in the war to frostbite. And heavily perfumed Aunt Toni with the gravelly voice. She wore loud charm bracelets, tempestuous gypsy blouses, and tiered dirndl skirts with petticoats underneath. Like Uncle Ken, Aunt Toni rolled her own cigarettes, except she used a little machine. Hers were much tidier. She walked with a glamorous limp and a fancy cane because of a motorcycle accident.

And let's not forget Betty's favourite, Auntie Muriel, her childhood pal. She worked as a policewoman in Northern Ireland. Auntie Muriel was living proof that you can wear red lipstick with a uniform and still be intimidating.

By contrast, there was gushy Aunt Sheila. She was more femmy and helpless than Aunt Muriel, as evidenced by the fact that she once broke her finger putting on her girdle.

Of all these ladies, Aunt Phyllis was my favourite. Paradoxically, she was the only one whose skull I fractured.

I vividly remember the day that Phyllis blew into our lives, like a lonely, disintegrating tumbleweed.

One afternoon in the late 1950s, I skipped home from primary school to find a forlorn-looking woman in a grey suit sitting in our living room. Though she was only in her 30s, her crumpled posture gave her the appearance of an old lady.

It was obvious that she was depressed, and even more obvious that she was blind. Helen Keller could have seen that she was blind. Some sightless people wear dark glasses to shield those around them from the drama of their handicap. Not Phyllis. She did not conceal her blindness with chic little sunglasses like Jane Wyman in

Magnificent Obsession. Everyone could see that Phyllis Robinson's eyes were missing. She had no eyeballs, and she did not care who knew it. In their place were two rather startling sunken pits.

Her accessories? A small, rhinestone, daisy lapel brooch, a sturdy handbag, a battered leather suitcase and a large female Labrador wearing a well-worn white leather harness.

My sister and I fell upon this beautiful golden beast, hugging her and playing with her massive silky ears.

'Phyllis and Lassie are going to be staying with us for a couple of weeks,' declaimed Betty by way of explanation. She lit up a Woodbine cigarette and shot my sister and me a look that discouraged the asking of moronic questions, adding, 'Just until she gets back on her feet, of course.'

As we played with Lassie's ears, twisting them into Austrian braided hairdos on the top of her head and making her look like a canine Hofbrau waitress, we had no idea that Phyllis was destined to stay for ten years, outlasting Uncle Ken, my crazy grandmother Narg and many of the other lodgers.

Though Betty was a tough-talking broad who professed to loathe do-gooders, she regularly found herself unable to resist the impulse to reach out and give a fellow human being a helping hand. Phyllis was in need of help.

'We have to take good care of her – she's addicted to purple hearts,' explained Betty in a hushed but matter-of-fact tone while Phyllis unpacked her meagre possessions.

These notorious pills were the preferred downers of the 1950s. Phyllis's addiction was causing her to lose her hair and parts of her mind. Betty had decided to rescue her.

Phyllis and Betty had only recently become friends. They had bonded while working for the same employers, a highly eccentric former White Russian prince and princess. This regal couple had been teenagers at the time of the revolution. Back in Russia they had lived in a luxurious, magical world of tinkly sleigh rides, Fabergé eggs, gilded samovars, and fur-trimmed Dostoevsky couture. And now, in an unbelievably perverse, excruciatingly cruel plot twist – probably one of the cruellest in the history of mankind – fate had plonked the royals down in Reading, our hometown, the least glamorous, dreariest place in the whole of Europe.

I have no idea how or why they ended up in the county of Berkshire, but I can tell you that the prince and princess faced the harsh economic realities of their new and appallingly lacklustre life with verve and creativity. The one thing they knew about was dogs. They had grown up surrounded by snow-white borzois and perfumed Afghans. They utilised their canine familiarities in the worthy task of training guide dogs for the blind, gaining a considerable notoriety in this field.

The guide dog business boomed. Paperwork proliferated. They hired stenographers like Phyllis and Betty from the local temp agency, Phyllis first and then Betty.

Once the women were in their clutches, the White

Russians commanded Betty and Phyllis to perform all kinds of nonsecretarial tasks, like hedge clipping, food serving, bath running, and toilet unblocking.

Adding to this eccentric working environment was the princess's pet monkey, who swung from the light fixtures, pooping on Betty and Phyllis, and taunting the lovely Lassie.

Betty adored the insane diversity of this experience. She talked ceaselessly and hilariously of the trials and tribulations of working for 'Ivan and Yvonne the Terrible'. She did a brilliant impersonation of the theatrical princess, duplicating a tone of voice which quivered and shook with tortured regret: 'I remember vashink my hairs wiz tventy-four eggs effry mornink while ze peasants outside ze palace were starfink.'

Phyllis's situation was far more complex. She was lodging full-time with the deposed nobles. Out of the blue, she developed a schoolgirl crush on the handsome prince. She became lovesick and wan. Her doctor – eager to write prescriptions for the latest antidepressants – prescribed purple hearts and more purple hearts. By the time Betty arrived, Phyllis was already knocking them back à la Neely O'Hara.*

One day the princess smelled a rat and gave Phyllis her marching orders. Distraught, Phyllis threw herself on Betty's mercy. Before you could sing 'Come On-a My

---

*I refer to the pill-popping, hellcat heroine in Jacqueline Susann's *Valley of the Dolls*.

House', Betty had offered her beleaguered pal a room *chez nous*.

Aunt Phyllis was installed in the one remaining space in our rambling, leaky red-brick Edwardian house. Her room was a windowless garret with a sloping ceiling on the top floor. It was freezing in the winter and boiling hot in the summer. Features included a non-opening skylight, a non-functioning fireplace, and an appropriately rock-bottom rent.

Despite her grim accommodations, Phyllis flourished. Under Betty's supervision, she put on weight, kicked the purple hearts, and learned to laugh again. A vigorous and not unattractive brunette rose from the ashes. It was a symbiotic arrangement: Betty now enjoyed the benefits of a live-in best friend and co-conspirator.

The 1960s arrived, and Phyllis and Betty embraced the concept of health food. They became ardent followers of the world's first granola guru, a Swiss bloke named Gayelord Hauser. Henceforth, every phrase uttered by Betty and Phyllis invariably contained the words *Gayelord Hauser*.

'Well, according to Gayelord Hauser, white sugar is white death.'

'Some chocolate cake? Just a thin slice. Don't tell Gayelord Hauser!'

On Saturdays, Phyllis and Betty would set out for the local health-food store – improbably named The High – and stock up on wheat germ, molasses, brewer's yeast, and anything else Gayelord Hauser was endorsing that particular week in his syndicated column.

An employee at The High convinced Betty that the key to health was growing your own greenery. In no time we had large plastic trays of sprouting bean shoots covering the sideboard in our dining room. Betty often tended them while enjoying a cigarette.

Thanks to Betty and Gayelord, the crumpled, depressed Phyllis morphed into a healthy, vibrant, singular being. She turned out to be more like a naughty big sister than an aunt.

The new Phyllis was an eccentric, courageous woman who made a mockery of her congenital handicap. Phyllis laughed when she walked into door frames or stepped in Lassie's poo. Blindness was a total gas! She loved to tell us about the time she exited a train on the wrong side, falling onto the tracks in a heap, *avec chien*.

The new Phyllis was also wildly unconventional. Her handicap afforded her a marginalised status, of which she now took full advantage. One day she came home in fits of laughter: she had, she explained, just returned from a very conventional tea party. One of the ladies present had an unruly dog. Exasperated, Phyllis had grabbed the dog and bitten it on the snout. With one nip she had subdued the dog and scared the hell out of the refined attendees.

Betty loved the new Phyllis. She was in heaven. She now had a chum with whom to cackle, someone to offset the psychotic ravings of our other lodgers.

The relationship between Betty and Phyllis was far more than that of landlady and lodger: they were two wildly opinionated broads who loved nothing more than an emotionally charged debate. Self-sacrificing, proud to be British, always ready for a verbal tussle, Phyllis was incapable of capitulating. Betty was similarly committed to her own world view, and equally nationalistic and feisty. Every night, the two would argue intensely with each other – over a bottle or two of banana-peel Château Doonan – mostly about what the English, i.e. Phyllis, had supposedly done to the non-English, i.e. Betty.

According to Betty, not only did the English lack a sense of fun but they were also completely and utterly devoid of imagination, flair and originality. They were, without exception, small-minded and stingy, and knew nothing about glamour. When they were poor they were pathetic, bitter and put-upon. Give them money or power and they became cruel, imperialist, hypocritical and grandiose. And if you doubted it, which one tended not to with Betty, she had a million examples, historic and contemporary, to prove her theses. Phyllis had no recourse but to defend herself and her country against grievous charges.

Their often incomprehensible and heated debates usually ended with Betty singing the national anthem and imitating the queen, while Phyllis screamed 'Rubbish!' with extra rolled *r*s.

~

My sister and I would never have dreamt of fighting with Aunt Phyllis. We worshipped and revered her. Every evening, we would accompany her to the Slope, a sharply angled public meadow where Lassie could run free. Here we would walk for hours with our favourite lodger, guiding her around piles of other dogs' poop. For some horrid reason, my memories of the dog poop on the Slope are very much intact. Much of it was white. I have no idea why. White dog poop seems to be a thing of the past. Maybe someday it will come back into style.

It was while returning from the poop-covered Slope that I fractured Phyllis's skull.

I was leading her down the street. We were chatting. She was correcting my pronunciation. All the kids at my rough, tough little school dropped their *h*s and *t*s. I was picking up the habit.

'You sound dreadfully common. There's an *h* in front of *horrible*, you know!' said Phyllis, castigating me at the top of her voice, thereby unwittingly castigating anyone common who was within earshot.

As we came towards a lamp post, I elected to skip around it, *à la* Gene Kelly in *Singin' in the Rain*. I assumed that Phyllis would make a corresponding move in the opposite direction. We would rehook our arms as soon as the obstacle had passed between us and continue on our merry way.

But Phyllis was blind.

So Phyllis kept walking, and then Phyllis smashed straight into the lamp post.

Her skull cracked into the forged steel post, making a sound that lives in the audio archives of my brain even unto this very day. It's filed under 'Cranial Destruction – Sound Effects'. If I were to Google the incident in my own brain, I would probably type in something like 'horribly shameful guilty skull crunching'.

The gonging noise echoed up and down the street. People stared at me reproachfully: 'You've killed a blind woman,' they seemed to say.

Phyllis swayed, groaning softly. I was about to ask her if she was 'seeing stars'. Fortunately I thought better of it.

I was dumbstruck with guilt and horror. My poor aunt Phyllis had dragged herself back from the brink – she had kicked purple hearts! – only to be murdered by her idiot nephew, who wasn't even a real nephew. I was terrified. Gayelord Hauser could not help her now. Even Lassie looked worried. We both waited for Phyllis to collapse to the ground. She twitched. I twitched.

I did not have the presence of mind to apologise. Since I had probably killed her, there did not really seem much point. It was too late for regrets.

She broke the painful silence.

'Not to worry!' said Phyllis, with the air of a woman who had slammed into worse things, and set off towards home.

By the time we reached our house, a massive lump had appeared on the front of her head, giving her the appearance of an exotic, prize-winning gourd.

'Oh maaay Goahwd!' said Betty, whose Belfast accent tended to resurface during times of stress.

'It's really nothing. I walked into a lamp post,' said Phyllis, not wanting to get me into trouble. 'I think I might just pop upstairs to the attic and lie down for a bit.'

Phyllis slept until the next morning. When she came down for her Gayelord Hauser-recommended breakfast, we all tried hard not to look at the gourd. Occasionally Phyllis would touch it and emit an 'Oooh!' of surprise. It was slightly larger than before.

The damage was never officially assessed. No doctors were ever consulted. A week later the gourd began to shrink. Six months later it was all but gone, leaving only a three-inch-long indentation.

Our forays to the Slope continued, but not without incident.

On more than one occasion, raincoat-wearing flashers ogled us from the bushes, taking cruel advantage of Aunt Phyllis's handicap.

'Lassie, whatever are you growling at?' Phyllis would say as the horrid, grinning men waved their rhubarb-coloured offerings in our direction.

My sister and I never said anything to Phyllis about these perverts. Why spoil a lovely evening?

At least the raincoat brigade kept their paws to them-selves. The same cannot be said of the horny hounds who regularly launched themselves at Lassie with such relent-less fervour. Phyllis took great pride in the fact that she had always successfully managed to defend Lassie against these would-be rapists.

On one vile and memorable occasion, she lost the battle.

One sunny evening a demonic black Baskerville hound leapt from the bushes. He fixed his gaze on the alluring Lassie and licked his lips. He then bounded towards us and jumped onto Lassie's back without so much as a 'Lovely weather we're having!' or a 'Do you come here often?'

We whacked the violator with tree branches and pelted him with conkers and insults. He began to jiggle his nasty jiggle. We screamed. Phyllis used bad language and thrashed him with Lassie's harness. Nothing could dislodge him. He looked quite happy. To make matters worse, so did Lassie.

'Run home and get your father, and don't stop at the sweet shop. Hurry!' commanded Phyllis.

I barrelled through the streets of Reading like a Pamplona person and burst into the living room.

'Dad! Lassie is – '

'Shhhhhhh! As soon as this is over.'

Terry was engrossed in watching *Z Cars*, a bi-weekly police drama which held the whole of early 1960s England in its thrall. As per his edict, I waited patiently until the

programme had finished. But it was already too late. As
the credits rolled, Shelagh and Aunt Phyllis were hurrying
in through the front gate, dragging Lassie, who was dragging her new boyfriend. This *tableau vivant* relieved me of
the need to explain the unexplainable.

Terry rushed outside and turned the hose on the
persistent fornicator. This made no difference. He kept on
doing his horrid jiggle.

Eventually fatigue set in, and probably hunger.
Lassie's lover jiggled to a stop and slid off her back. He
then loped off down the street without so much as a 'We
really must do this more often', or even a 'Thanks, luv!'

Terry was suitably mortified. He apologised profusely
for stifling my attempts to communicate and for prioritis-
ing his TV watching over defending Lassie against rape.

Nobody seemed inclined to discuss that horrid
jiggling. Nobody seemed to have the right words to
describe what had occurred. Or the inclination. Jiggling
was embarrassing and animalistic and strange. Jiggling
involved violence, chaos and mayhem. No wonder ladies
like Phyllis chose not to jiggle.

Years passed. Phyllis thrived. Lassie died and was
succeeded by various less glamorous varmints. Eventually,
Betty decided to give all the lodgers their marching orders.
She needed a break from washing people's undies and
cutting up Phyllis's food into bite-sized morsels, which
she did religiously and uncomplainingly for years.

When Betty gave Phyllis notice to move out, the latter dissolved into tears and hid in her garret. Half a bottle of turnip wine later, she had adjusted to the idea.

Within a matter of weeks, Phyllis relocated to an asbestos bungalow – with no ill effects – where we and other members of her family were regular visitors.

She never married or jiggled with anyone, as far as I know. Her dogs were the loves of her life. Whenever one of them died, it sent her into a spiral of grief which I have yet to witness in any human bereavement. Fortunately, her last dog – a black Lab called Barney, named after my employer – outlived her. At the time of her death, aged 89, she was the oldest living guide dog owner on record.

When I heard of Phyllis's death and imminent interment, all I could think about was the time she and Lassie (who should probably have had her eyes tested) fell into an open grave at a friend's funeral. She came home with bloodied knees and grass in her hair. She could hardly get the story out she was laughing so hard.

Chapter 6

CAMP

'THERE'S a lovely bar called the Beachcomber,' said Cyril Biddlecombe with excessive gravity, 'and they have a tropical rainstorm every twenty minutes.'

'It's a tape recording,' said Biddie, nudging me in the ribs and rolling his eyes.

It is the summer of 1962. I am going on vacation with the Biddlecombe family. We are travelling to the county of Somerset to spend not one but two weeks at the Butlins Holiday Camp located in the ominously named town of Minehead, a former swamp.

Sir William Edmund Butlin (1899–1980) started out

working at a fun fair. His mission in life was the creation of a leisure culture for working-class folk. Prior to his innovation, the sulky proletariat spent their pre-global-warming holidays cowering from the driving rain in wind-lashed bus shelters at smelly coastal resorts. Then along came Butlins, a bright, shrill, plastic, thigh-slapping, Technicolor antidote to the grim reality of factory life. By the time Biddie and I are disembarking at Minehead train station, Butlins, with its überjolly uniformed 'Redcoat' camp counsellors, is an established institution.

Biddie is a Butlins veteran, albeit of the less enthusiastic variety. He has visited most of the camps in the United Kingdom but is ready to ditch the Butlins experience for a bit of Euro-sophistication.

'Monte Carlo is supposed to be lovely at this time of year,' he muses as we pull into the train station.

From the moment we arrive at the Minehead Camp, I am totally overwhelmed. The unflinching commitment to fun hits me like a tidal wave. Everybody at Butlins seems to be screeching his head off with manic glee. Here are all the grim-faced Eleanor Rigbys of England, and they are actually having fun. It is quite terrifying.

I demand to see the Beachcomber Bar. We dump our suitcases in our 'chalets' – underfurnished, mustard-yellow, cell-like rooms containing bunk beds and no discernible connection to Switzerland – and head over to catch the first tropical rainstorm.

The Beachcomber Bar is located inside what appears to

be a brightly painted, recycled World War II aeroplane hangar. All the Butlins attractions are similarly housed.

We enter. I gasp. The dreary exterior is a fantastically successful foil for the insanely overdecorated interior. Every surface is covered with AstroTurf and bamboo-printed vinyl. Plastic palm fronds and succulents billow from every direction, creating a womblike jungle ambience.

A sturdy waitress wearing a garland of fake orchids waddles over to our table.

'A Babycham, please,' says Doreen Biddlecombe, ordering the latest ladylike beer alternative.

'Nothing for the kids,' says Cyril, 'a pint for me. By the way, when is the tropical rainstorm due?'

'Oops!' says the waitress and scurries off behind a palm tree. She flicks a switch and – bingo! Thunder. Lightning. Instant tropical rainstorm.

Biddie and I exchange glances. We look around the jungle at the people enjoying their drinks. Here they are, in the middle of a former swamp in a large metal shed which has been stapled with tons and tons of plastic greenery, and they are acting *as if* they are in Hawaii.

This is a transformative moment for both of us.

In one blinding flash we understand the meaning of *camp*.

The extreme atmosphere and decor of the Beachcomber Bar unleashed in us a correspondingly extreme theatricality. From that moment forwards, every second of every day at Butlins presented us with some fresh and irresistible opportunity for *exaggeration*. The excess of Butlins demanded full-blown demonstrations of uninhibited enjoyment from us, and we were only too happy to oblige. As we sat in the Beachcomber Bar, we automatically found ourselves emulating the poses and animated expressions of people who might be enjoying a tropical hideaway. The minute we adopted the corny body language of happy holidaymakers, we *became* those happy holidaymakers.

Finding out that we could do things *as if* we were doing them was, for Biddie and me, a transcendental and highly addictive discovery. Entering a room *as if* one was entering a room was so much more amusing and exhilarating than just entering a room. This revelation opened the door to a squishy, dark, velvet-lined place in our respective psyches.

From that moment on we luxuriated in the cut-price, cheesy pathos of the relentlessly upbeat Butlins experience. We had so much more fun because we were behaving *as if* we were having fun.

It was pure *camp*, literally and figuratively. Effortlessly we nudged and winked our way through the entire rainy holiday. In this desperate hothouse of frenzied kitsch, our camp sensibilities blossomed and flourished and fed off each other. We may not have been sun-drenched, but we were definitely irony-drenched.

We sang along enthusiastically with the wakey-wakey breakfast song (piped directly into our chalets). We cheered the infantile games and endless talent contests. We smiled appreciatively at the gaudiness and schlockiness of the amusements and the decor.

The epicentre of Butlins was the monumental indoor swimming pool. The entire ceiling was draped with all manner of plastic festoonery: fake birds, leafy plastic vines and tropical flowers. Every expense was spared. Though the tepid water was treacherously chlorinated and hair, mucus and plasters clogged the gutters, we neither noticed nor cared. We were too busy acting *as if* we were in a Busby Berkeley movie.

I can remember, as if it were yesterday, Biddie's sister Sheila frolicking in this exotic environment in a bikini with red and black horizontal stripes. She looked like a bumblebee with Fascist leanings. While running round the pool, she slipped and fell, bouncing into the water like a beach ball. I have never seen such slapstick before or since.

More kitsch lurked underwater. Below ground, the pool was cunningly recessed into an endless, linoleum-floored tea room. Large windows looked directly into the underwater murk. The glass-topped occasional tables at which we campers sat contained mounds of fluorescent-lit plastic flowers. Here we consumed cups of tea and shrimp-paste sandwiches while watching – through vignettes of plastic corals and Vac-U-Form plastic fish – the semi-clad bodies of our fellow holidaymakers.

There was clearly something disgustingly voyeuristic about the whole arrangement. There were always a few suspect-looking older geezers lingering over their crisps waiting for some pale-skinned nymph to plop into view.

Biddie told me that many of the Butlins camps had this fabulous and outrageously kinky architectural feature. The Biddlecombes loved to recall the occasion when Cyril's square-cut wool swimming trunks descended to his ankles, in full view of a cackling crowd.

After a lazy day by the pool, Doreen and Cyril would, as often as not, retreat to the smoke-filled Pig and Whistle, where plastic salamis and jokes on plaques festooned the ceiling.

> My wife's gone to the West Indies.
> Jamaica?
> No, she went of her own accord!

Much as we adored reading the plaques and watching the adults getting smashed in these themed watering holes, we did not linger.

'We have a show to catch,' we would announce in a rather grand theatrical manner. Biddie and I then headed over to the Butlins Playhouse. It wasn't love of the dramatic arts that took us there. It was sadism. We adored nothing more than watching the exhausted Butlins thespians slogging their way through dramatised versions of Agatha Christie and the like, as if they were in some Broadway smash. These turgid productions were poorly attended. As a result we always seemed to have front-row seats.

One evening in particular stands out. On this occasion Biddie and I were thoroughly transfixed by a stout, mature lady who delivered her lines like a parody of a stout mature lady. Her bust jiggled, and saliva shot from her mouth, onto us, as she denounced her errant son. Bringing her monologue to a thundering crescendo, she flung herself into the nearest armchair.

Unfortunately for her, she missed her target and ended up pinioned on the pointy arm of her chair. The surprised expression on her face and the squeal she emitted indicated that this manoeuvre was not in the script.

Already in an excitable state, Biddie and I went into paroxysms of uncontrollable laughter. Like the object of our mockery, Biddie and I were also a little stout. As a result, our wobbling and poorly muffled giggling proved quite distracting. Eventually the old trouper tired of our derision. She took a huge breath. Leaning forwards, and breaking the magical membrane between audience and performer, she screamed 'Do shut up!' directly into our chubby, petrified faces.

Butlins was theatrical, camp and kitsch, but it was also, on occasion, a tad louche.

Though prepubescent, we became feverish aficionados of the seedy underbelly of camp life. Tacky Butlins seemed like the opposite of the wholesome American summer camps I had read about, with their frantic canoeing, flag-raisings and tepees.

'I think she's one of the rides,' quipped Biddie's sister as we spied through the bushes on a female camper with a rock-hard beehive hairdo, yellow boots and fishnets. This lady clearly spent her holidays, beer and fag in hand, flirting shamelessly with passers-by from her chalet threshold. It was nice to know that freewheeling single gals could afford Butlins too.

Slags and cocktails were about the only things not included in the cost. All the theatrical entertainments, meals, fairground rides, and cheesy variety shows were 'free'.

Toilet paper was, for some reason, not included in the cost. I had been warned about this and brought my own roll with me. At any given time you could spot a holiday-maker or two sprinting through the rain, clutching a loo roll, on his or her way to communal toilets (known as 'the bogs'). This gave Butlins the feeling of a minimum security correctional facility, as did the razor wire which topped off the incredibly high chain-link perimeter fencing.

Potential freeloaders were said to be a constant threat at Butlins. Biddie and I were greatly amused by the idea of desperate fun seekers breaking into Butlins and availing themselves of the facilities like crazed drug addicts. By the beginning of the second week of our stay, we were bored with mocking the kitsch of Butlins and moved on to more sinister territory. We began to speculate about the strict security measures: were they designed to keep *them* out, or *us* in?

We developed all kinds of extreme persecution scenarios and renamed our camp Butlitz. The communal bathrooms became 'delousing stations', and the chalets were our 'bunkers'. We started to speak with German accents and pretend to quote from *Mein Kampf.* The famous Butlins Redcoat counsellors were no longer genial hosts but psychopathic camp commandants.

Biddie and I took great pleasure in spreading vile rumours to other kids about what the Butlitz Redcoats did to people who were reluctant to participate in the nonstop *fun*!

'Ve heff vays of mekking you loff!' Biddie would say as he jackbooted round our chalet/bunker. When we saw a Redcoat heading in our direction, we would throw him or her off our scent by hooting with laughter and skipping about.

I was familiar with the horror of the Holocaust. Blind Aunt Phyllis had a good friend called Inge who had survived Auschwitz. The experience had left her orphaned, partially sighted and profoundly traumatised. Inge also had a bad case of arrested development. Dressed like a little girl, with white ankle socks and a bow in her hair, she would sit for hours in our living room with a cold cup of tea on her knee. Betty did not mince words about what had happened to poor Inge during the war.

'Be nice to her!' she would command, adding, in case we thought of doing otherwise, 'Her whole family went up the chimney in Auschwitz. Bloody Krauts! Thank God we won the war!'

Thank God there were no Inges at Butlins to witness our hideous behaviour.

Our perverse fun came screeching to a halt when we both succumbed to food poisoning. I can still remember the dodgy-looking lard-fried eggs that brought it on. The virulence of the attack was made all the more hideous by the fact that we had to schlep to the communal toilets/delousing stations in order to throw up, etc.

Maintaining our new-found sense of irony while suffering through food poisoning was quite difficult, but somehow we managed. I distinctly remember attempting to throw up *as if* I was throwing up.

Food poisoning was far from rare at Butlins. This was, I hasten to add, back in the days before *E. coli* came into common parlance and hand washing became a national pastime. None of the Redcoats seemed remotely surprised or apologetic when they encountered groups of groaning, stomach-clutching campers. They treated food poisoning as if it were one of the rides in the amusement park. Our turn had come. Lucky us.

I must emphasise that these recollections about the Butlins of my formative years should not be construed as a commentary on the Butlins of today which, I might add, remains a perfectly marvellous holiday option.

The gastric agonies eventually subsided, and we both made full Piaf-like recoveries. We had no regrets. Our time at Butlins had been positively life changing.

Biddie and I had discovered Camp.

Butlins did not seem to have this effect on everyone. Not everyone at Minehead was posing in doorways or bursting over the side of the swimming pool with such studied enthusiasm. This perplexed us. Biddie and I did not understand how people could be so utterly doltish and boring in such an environment. How can you dive in an artless, doltish, ramshackle kind of way into a swimming pool which has been painstakingly festooned with plastic birds and flowers? It is insulting to the swimming pool itself and to all the good people who have tried so feverishly to give you the Esther Williams experience of a lifetime.

You must walk to the end of the diving board, suck in your stomach and your cheeks, raise your arms like Evita, and dive with the self-consciousness and panache of somebody who understands that life is a stage set, a really tacky, faded stage set.

Thanks to our two weeks in Minehead, Biddie and I now acted exactly like the people in the Butlins postcards and brochures. We had found ourselves, or at least the waving, posing brochure versions of ourselves.

Chapter 7

GUTS

E VERYWHERE I looked there were sets of rose-pink dentures soaking in mugs or drinking glasses. False teeth were a huge part of my childhood and of the landscape of the 20th century. No slapstick movie or TV comedy sketch was complete without a set of chattering dentures. It is no exaggeration to say that false teeth were *culturally central*.

Having all one's teeth pulled out was not just inevitable, it was positively de rigueur! When Betty, still in her 30s, announced that her denture days had arrived, nobody in our house batted an eyelid. We saw it as a happy happenstance: soon our already glamorous mother would have a fabulous new smile. How could it be anything other than a totally life-enhancing change?

We were woefully unprepared for the overwhelming hideousness of the whole ordeal. When Betty returned home from the dentist, a cerise-coloured chiffon head-scarf wound tightly around her head and jaw, she looked as if she had been in a car accident. Not only did she look dreadful, but she also carried about her the sad and hope-less air of a broken woman. What on Earth had happened? Where was that glamorous Lana Turner confi-dence we had all come to know and love?

Betty shuffled to the sideboard and poured herself a glass of gin. She took a half-hearted sip. The liquid drib-bled out of her mouth. She abandoned her glass and then lit a cigarette. It fell poignantly from her unrouged lips. She was Lana Turner all right, only it was the downtrodden Madame X she was playing as opposed to the upbeat as-sertive Lora in *Imitation of Life*.

Betty collapsed on the couch and stared at the ceiling. Her lips caved in slightly. She now resembled the hideous toothless gypsy hags who banged on our front door once a week and menaced us into buying their malfunctioning clothes pegs.

Simultaneously, my sister and I burst into tears.

So began a gruesome and interminable period of toothlessness while we all waited for Betty's gums to heal and for the arrival of her new choppers.

Though bloody and bruised, Betty received little sympathy. I was unapologetically furious with her for looking so horrid and unattractive. My sister shared my indignation and continued to weep openly and reproachfully. Narg and Uncle Ken and Aunt Phyllis and Terry had all gone through same thing. They had received sympathy. But Betty was different. She had an obligation to us. Glamour was part of her contract.

Eventually the new choppers arrived. Betty, with a gleaming set of movie-star white teeth, was back to her old self again and then some. We breathed easy.

A minor challenge now presented itself. The new Hollywood teeth did not seem to fit as well as they might. It took only a light sneeze to send Betty's gnashers flying across the kitchen. I can still recall the poignant noise they produced when they hit various hollow surfaces and rattled to the floor.

Flying dentures were a common sight back then. Nobody in our house seemed able to keep choppers in place for any length of time. Sneezing and coughing were the most common cause. The sequence was as follows.

'Achew!'

Rattling sound.

'Oh, Christ!' (Spoken in toothless voice.)

Whenever Betty's teeth flew out, we looked away until she popped them back in. If Terry was the culprit, we gave ourselves full permission to enjoy the slapstick. I still chuckle when I recall the day his choppers landed in the oil under his motorbike.

Undeterred by Betty's oral crucifixion, I began to crave my own set of dentures. My reasoning was simple. Once I had dentures, I would no longer be obliged to visit Mr Porter. He was our large and terrifying dentist, whose unmarried, one-armed sister functioned as his assistant. He drilled our teeth, sans anaesthetic, with a device that looked like a vintage Black & Decker. While the sadist drilled, his sister held us down with her one arm.

The agonised shrieks that rose from his chair caused much weeping and sighing among adults and children alike as they trembled in the adjacent waiting room.

When my sister and I expressed any fear of Mr Porter, Betty became rather uneasy. She could not cope with the idea that she might be raising children with low pain thresholds. Cowardice of any kind was absolutely unacceptable. She would have preferred that we become drug addicts or shoplifters. Anything was preferable to being yellow.

Betty's side of the family was very, very butch. She came from a tough clan of pain-loving Northern Irish Protestants.

'Your grandmother just had her varicose veins cut, and she refused painkillers,' she proudly announced one day, daring us to react. Her reasoning was as follows: anaesthetics were for weaklings and English people. The Northern Irish had a higher tolerance for pain because they had endured suffering and because they were much, much, much better people.

When my grandfather wrote to Betty informing her that he and his wife had just removed what were left of each other's teeth with electrical pliers, Betty waved the letter aloft as if it were a winning lottery ticket.

I began to be slightly concerned. What would happen if I ever got drastically sick? I could just imagine Betty holding back the anaesthetist as I underwent an appendectomy or a heart transplant. 'Don't be ridiculous! Of course he doesn't need any Demerol. He's of Northern Irish descent!'

Once a year we had the opportunity to visit the primordial slime from which all this tough-guy stuff emerged. Every July we decamped to strife-torn Belfast to visit Betty's father.

David Carson Gordon was a member of an unusually butch species. He is long dead and his species is now extinct, but it used to be quite common. I saw specimens on every street corner in Northern Ireland.

I guess you could call them Irish working-class boulevardiers. They were easy to spot because, like Amish or Hasidim, they had a very specific personal style. Their jaunty appearance was an amalgam of country and city style, reflecting the contradictions of their formerly rural lives.

Having come from the wilds of County Antrim, DC Gordon was a prime example of this genre of small-town tough guy. Attired in a collarless shirt and a mud-flecked, thick wool, pinstriped, three-piece suit, he cut an impressive figure as he squinted down at the gold watch and chain that dangled from his waistcoat. His trousers were tucked into a pair of dark green, poo-spattered rubber wellies. His meticulously combed, centre-parted hair – very Edwardian – was covered by a flat farmer's tweed cap. It was all very proto-Ralph Lauren.

These dandies were not to be found in England. I saw men like DC Gordon only in Northern Ireland. The fellows back home were, by comparison, quite wimpy and pathos-drenched. They wore thick glasses and depressing cardigans from Marks & Spencer – very Ted Heath – and their hair was Brylcreemed into stripy comb-overs. They could often be seen meekly accompanying their wives on shopping trips up the local high street.

Compared to these neutered males, DC and his cronies were swashbuckling pirates or libidinous musketeers.

There were invariably gaggles of these gentlemen lurking outside the Belfast pubs and betting shops. They had the air of men who were charged with making important, world-altering decisions. As they chatted, glancing up and down the street, they gave the impression that deep thoughts and momentous ideas were being exchanged, as opposed to, for example, racing tips.

These tough guys had their own florid and scary language. They entertained each other with hilariously creative similes and euphemisms. If he thought somebody was tightfisted, DC would say of that person, 'Him! He'd drink beer out of a shitey rag, as long as someone else is payin'.'

If a male friend was married to a harridan and that friend happened to drop dead, DC would sum up the situation with a laconic, 'He preferred the boards.' These kinds of remarks were usually followed by toothless cackles of auto-amusement.

While the men were thus engaged, the womenfolk bustled to and fro, doing pointless, self-indulgent things like child rearing, food gathering, ignoring their aches and pains, and generally depriving themselves in order to make ends meet. No wonder Betty had run off to join the air force and married a bloke who rubbed her feet and listened to opera.

In DC's world, men had a full monopoly on recreational activities. While the women scrubbed and toiled and baked without so much as a pinch on the bum or a thank you, their menfolk seemed unable to function without a steady flow of time-honoured pleasures and rewards. They were hardworking, but only in sporadic bursts. The rest of the time they gambled on the horses and drank Guinness and cultivated audaciously high expectations of their womenfolk. They were completely and utterly heterosexual.

I have a great snapshot of DC sitting proudly in a horse-drawn cart with his name emblazoned across the front. This image recalls Charlton Heston's chariot-racing scene in *Ben-Hur*. At the time of the snap, DC was the

proprietor of a thriving milk delivery business. This enter-
prise – the apotheosis of his career – eventually failed.
According to Betty, the reasons were twofold: first, and
commendably, good-hearted DC had a hard time collecting
money from the poor and gave away much of the milk.
Second, and less fabulously, what little profits were made
went straight to the betting shop or the cash register at
the Woodman's Arms.

The life of a Northern Irish boulevardier was not without its challenges. On one occasion, while sauntering
home from the aforementioned Woodman's Arms after an
evening of conviviality, a 65-year-old DC plunged into a
construction hole, breaking a leg and losing a great deal of
dignity. He was carted off to hospital, where the fractured
limb was encased in plaster. Painkillers were ostenta-
tiously declined. DC was then told that he must rest for
two months. The phrase 'never walk again' was used.

Poo-pooing these warnings, DC discharged himself
and staggered home. Heading directly to the toolshed, he
set about removing the massive cast with a hacksaw. It
was thirsty work. Free of the cast, he hobbled back to the
Woodman's Arms. Propping himself up at the bar, he
regaled his cohorts with his adventure. The Guinness
flowed. Everybody, Betty included, marvelled at his
unmedicated bravery.

Within his community, DC, the handsome widower,
was considered to be not only gutsy but eligible. Various
local ladies had their eyes on him. Coiffed and perfumed,

they would drop by to flirt and partake of tea. His favourite way to discourage this kind of behaviour was to lie on the floor with the lights out. My sister and I enjoyed this charade. We had read Anne Frank's newly published *Diary of a Young Girl*. We knew what to do.

If the widows caught us all in the front yard, DC would switch to Plan B. This entailed making tea and feeding the unwanted visitors ancient slices of bread from his chicken feed bin. My sister and I took great delight in watching this ritual.

'Davey, is this bread no' a wee bit mouldy?' his coquettish lady friends would ask as they stared anxiously at the small, furry, grey-green blotches.

'Notatall! Sure, it's fresh the daaay!' he would reply, daring them, with his handsome dark-brown eyes, not to partake.

These moments of hilarity were few and far between. Most of the time DC was a grunty and remote host.

This is probably a good moment to reflect on the tour de force that was Betty Doonan née Gordon. Most of her year was spent toiling, mothering, cutting up blind Aunt Phyllis's food, and contending with Narg and Ken, our schizophrenic live-in relatives. The only respite from this routine was our annual holiday, out of the frying pan and into Northern Ireland. While we frolicked in the icy, oily waters of Belfast Lough, Betty cooked and scrubbed and attempted to alleviate the squalor of her eccentric and demanding parent. Well-coiffed, maquillaged and uncomplaining, she confronted these familial challenges head-on.

My mum had long since reconciled herself to the fact that relatives were nothing but trouble. For Betty they were synonymous with dreadful goings-on, drudgery and emotional turmoil. If she ever heard that a friend or colleague was expecting a visit from an in-law, there was always a sharp intake of breath followed by a sympathetic glance and the offering of a consoling cigarette. I inherited this trait. To this day when people announce the imminent arrival of grandparents or cousins, it's hard for me to restrain myself from saying, 'Oh, God, I'm really sorry. Let me know if there is anything I can do, and know that I'm there for you during this dark and horrible period.'

The role played by nicotine should not be underestimated. Betty's coping skills were bolstered and sustained by a heavy and not unreasonable reliance on cigarettes. Betty's complex life was never going to afford her long stretches of thigh-slapping fun. She took her releases and recreations in small, wry increments. These lasted about as long as it takes to smoke a cigarette. Woodbines were her preferred brand. Like Betty herself, Woodbines were short, strong and tough. Once she was back on Irish soil, her Woodbine consumption quadrupled.

More often than not we arrived for our annual holiday to find DC going to or coming from a wake. Funerals loomed large on DC's calendar. He took them seriously. They were the only time he bothered to wear his false teeth. These occasions became increasingly frequent as he got older. 'Guess who's dead?' he would say upon returning home from a day at the pub, indicating that those dusty dentures were due for an outing.

After the initial guarded but warm hellos – there were no California hugs or European air kisses back then – old resentments would eventually float to the surface. DC had never quite forgiven Betty for leaving Northern Ireland and, worse still, marrying an Englishman.

Betty had barely stubbed out the first ciggie before DC began to assert himself. His favourite method of control involved blood and death. Strolling casually into the backyard, he would murder about three or four chickens in quick succession. The fowl in question ran around freely. He would wring their necks and shove them into an oil drum with the same nonchalance that other people straighten their ties or touch up their lipstick. He would then disappear to the pub. Betty was left to pluck, gut, truss and cook them in the ancient, tiny, malfunctioning oven which raged in DC's closet-sized kitchen.

When he returned from the pub, he would kill another one.

'He's murdering them faster than I can gut them!' lamented Betty with her hand up a chicken's bum, *à la* glove puppet.

DC's chickens were the focus of much of his daily life. He ate their eggs raw every morning, tossing the shells with chilling accuracy over his shoulder and directly into the fire. He also reared pheasants and ducks and grew his own veggies. The only thing he seemed to buy from a store was bread. Everything else was grown or raised in his guano-filled urban backyard. He built wire enclosures for his birds with his bare hands and dragged home heavy feed bags in the pouring rain. Even in his 70s he remained tough and invincible. Normal men seemed unbelievably nelly when compared to DC.

DC was the anti-nelly. He was the opposite of me. I found him unbelievably intimidating and kept my distance. We had nothing to talk about. His lack of teeth and his heavily accented, grunty speech kept communication to a minimum. I could never have shared with him my burgeoning love of fashion and decorative accessories. His Guinness-addled world view did not encompass the Beautiful People. We existed in separate dimensions of time and space and beauty.

When I reached the age of ten I noticed a marked change. DC started to look at me differently. He began to size me up as if he was planning something. I felt uneasy. Maybe he was going to throttle me or take me to market.

One day he brought me and my sister, Shelagh, to visit a friend of his who kept ponies. We spent an afternoon cantering and trotting around his paddock, observed by DC and his cohort. They admired our form and complimented us on our skill. When I fell off, DC gathered me up and plonked me back in the saddle. Here at last were the glimmerings of the kind of rapport which all my friends seemed to have with their grandparents. My sister was definitely a better rider than I, but, for some strange reason, DC was focusing his attention on me.

All was revealed when we got home.

'The wee lad would make a fine jockey, so he would!' announced DC to Betty, who, as usual, had her hand up a chicken's bum.

He was right about one thing. I was definitely wee. And I wasn't getting any taller. But those weren't doting grandfatherly glints of commiseration in his eyes. They were dollar signs. Suddenly I felt the cold draft of exploitation blowing up my wee jodhpur leg.

(*Wee* remains an important word to this day. On a recent trip, I dragged a reluctant Terry, now a widower, to the Belfast branch of Marks & Spencer to replenish his socks and undies. It was a bitterly cold but sunny day. I was wearing a belted trench coat, a fur hat and dark glasses. I was channelling Betty in both the bossiness of my behaviour and the drama of my attire.

As I waited on line at the checkout, a large, red-faced Irish lady tried to push in front of me. 'Let the wee lady go first!' said the checkout gal, indicating me. Terry said nothing. I did, however, notice a wry smile curling the corners of his lips.)

Having established that I was a 'wee boy' with money-earning potential, DC lost no time in educating Betty about the most effective ways to stunt my growth.

'A little nip of gin in his milk will do the trick,' he said, causing everyone to guffaw with laughter as if he was joking, which of course he wasn't.

With a twanging of springs, DC plonked himself down on his battered two-seater leather couch. Placing a massive paw on each armrest, he began to drum out a tattoo with his fingers. He stared into the middle distance. I could tell he was having a wildly premature fantasy about me. I was toying with the same fantasy.

I'm racing in the Grand National. I'm wearing a fetching ensemble of yellow and red satin. DC is cheering me on.

It's a dramatic race. At the very last moment I surge into the lead and win by a hair.

I'm borne aloft by DC.

It's time to accept my trophy.

DC inserts his dentures in preparation to meet the queen. (The queen is already wearing hers.) Now he's lifting me onto a box so that Her Majesty can present me with a large silver cup. I hand the trophy back to DC for safekeeping.

DC starts to snore. The fantasy comes to an abrupt halt.

~

I managed to dodge my grandfather's various schemes, equestrian and otherwise. When I reached five feet, three inches, he gave up on the jockey scenario. His goals for me became more modest. He wanted to live long enough to see me reach the age when he could drag me to the pub and teach me to drink.

Maybe it was fortunate for us both that he did not live long enough to accompany me to a pub and watch me ordering a crème de menthe or a pink lady.

When he finally popped his clogs, we decamped to Northern Ireland to sort through his things. While Terry wheeled barrowloads of empty bottles back to the liquor store, Betty sifted through a shoebox of papers and assessed the financial situation. An early proponent of the concept of 'spending down', DC had skillfully managed to die with a zero bank balance. In my mother's family, most people had the decency to die with enough money in the bank to pay for their own interment. Gramps was more laissez-faire.

After a couple of Woodbines and an epiphany of lateral thinking, Betty painted her lips, picked up her handbag, threw on her leather trench, and caught the bus into town. Shielding her complex coiffure from the gusting Belfast Lough winds with the aid of her bag, she strode up the high street to the Woodman's Arms, the pub into which her father had haemorrhaged his pension. Ensconcing herself in the 'snug' – the anteroom designated for females while the men drank in the main saloon – she ordered a gin and tonic. When the proprietor came to pay his respects, Betty calmly went in for the kill. She pulled the undertaker's bill out of her purse and hit him up for the money to bury her father. And she got it.

I hope she never paid it back, but, knowing her, I'm sure she did.

★

★

★

Chapter 8

GIFTS

I HAVE an auntie Marigold and an uncle Vivian. She is a redhead. He is not a woman.

During the early part of the last century, it was not uncommon for male children to be named Vivian. Boys were also named Evelyn and Jocelyn, Lyndsey, or even Beverly. I can offer no explanation.

But Uncle Vivian is not weird. Despite the fact that he came from a family of certified lunatics, my dad's brother is quite abnormally normal. He even belongs to a golf club. Vivian is a traditionalist. Having spent a gruelling childhood contending with Narg, his poor deranged mother – hauling her out of the gas oven was among his regular chores – Vivian worked hard to achieve a life of prosperity and stability.

Uncle Vivian and Auntie Marigold were always big on Christmas. Their philosophy was as follows: every child in the family, no matter how vile or bratty, was eligible for a gift right up until the magical moment when he or she got married. Marriage signified the passing of the Xmas baton, when the responsibilities of gift-giving mystically transferred themselves to the firm young shoulders of the newly-weds. Marriage confirmed one's status as an adult and disqualified one, in a totally positive kind of way, from a place on Marigold's gift list.

This system worked well, until my sister and I came along. Let me rephrase that. This system worked well until my lesbian sister and I came along.

Between us, Shelagh Doonan and I managed not only to deconstruct this system but also to place a lingering strain on the yuletide budgets of our well-meaning aunt and uncle. We threw a spanner in the works. We buggered up the system. We refused to play ball. Neither of us got married until we reached middle age, and then it was to people of our own gender.

In fairness to all concerned, my sister and I have never been what you'd call easy to buy for.

It started when we were tiny tots.

~

One frosty Saturday in December, handsome Uncle Vivian
appeared bearing gifts. He opened his manly traveling
valise and, with a grand 'voilà!', presented my sister with
a doll named Sally Anne.

Sally Anne was special. Sally Anne wore a crunchy frock
of flower-printed tulle. When you rocked her, she gurgled.
Her eyelids then lowered, giving her a strange, blissed-out
expression.

Shelagh reacted violently but not unreasonably. She
did what any self-respecting, four-year-old lesbian-in-
the-making would have done, she attempted to murder
Sally Anne.

Sally Anne hit the skirting board with a sickening
crunching sound, skidded about four feet, and disappeared
under a bed. Uncle Vivian was too engrossed in conversation to notice Shelagh hurling Sally Anne across the room
with all her might. Betty and Terry were preoccupied with
being festive and yuletidey. Nobody saw. Nobody cared.

But I saw, and I cared. I cared a lot.

Deeply moved by the plight of this unwanted innocent, I crawled in under the bed and retrieved her. The
damage was significant. Her head was cracked. One dislo-
cated arm dangled two inches lower than the other.

I pulled her frock down off her head and made her decent again. Cradling her and stroking her marcel-waved
rayon hair, I attempted to make the pain go away. I vowed
to nurse Sally Anne back to health. Under my care she
would learn to gurgle again.

Eventually, once she was back on her feet, I would effect an entente cordiale between Sally Anne and Shelagh.

'She was just playing. She didn't mean to hurt you,' I said, kissing her linoleum-grazed cheek. 'She loves you. Really she does.'

But I knew in my heart that it was a lie. Shelagh loathed Sally Anne. Like any right-thinkin' tomboy, my sister had homicidal feelings towards this doll and all dolls. Dolls were girlie and stupid and contemptible. Shelagh was far more interested in my toys, in particular the butch little toy truck Uncle Vivian had just assigned to me. And as far as I was concerned, she was welcome to it. I hated that truck as much as she hated Sally Anne.

The Sally Anne debacle was a watershed incident. From this moment on, neither one of us exhibited any of the conventional tastes of our gender. We were gender-confused, but happily so.

Our unorthodox tastes formed the basis of a strange symbiosis. We traded gifts like baseball cards.

Me: I'll give you this toy aeroplane if you'll give me your plastic lacy parasol.

Shelagh: I'll give you my rag doll, the one in the gingham dress with the two rows of rickrack on the hem, if you'll give me your toy shovel.

What did our parents make of this transgender trend? Please remember, dear reader, that these incidents occurred long before the contemporary hysteria surrounding childhood. Back in the 1950s, parents were infinitely less focused on their children's development. As long as we did not exhibit signs of schizophrenia, Betty and Terry were quite happy.

As I grew older and the gifts got more butch, my motivation to get rid of them increased, as did Shelagh's motivation to tear them from my limp grasp. What a relief it was to offload all those dreary toy aeroplanes, especially the annoying plastic ones I was supposed to enjoy assembling myself! I can still recall the dizziness and euphoria caused by the highly intoxicating adhesive that came with each kit. The glue high was, in fact, the only thing that made assembling these aeroplanes bearable. How many poor gay boys have become glue sniffers in order to withstand the tedium of building those bloody aeroplanes?

Though we enjoyed a happy and unique arrangement, it was not always smooth sailing. For example, when we played Cowboys and Indians we were not quite sure how to divvy up the roles. Somehow my sister, being older and more conniving, persuaded me that the Indian braves, with their long hair, shift dresses and penchant for beads, were actually women. This changed my entire outlook. I happily became an Indian. This set her free to become a gun-wielding *Bonanza* type. Little Joe was her favourite.

And then there were the fairies. I know it sounds preposterous, but we actually *played fairies*. This was not some idiosyncrasy born of my nelly ways. We, along with all the other uncorrupted innocents of our generation, believed in Peter Pan and Alice in Wonderland. In our house, where many of the adults seemed to occupy an alternative reality, what was a fairy or two? We – even Shelagh, who at about this time developed a strange habit of referring to herself as Jim – were always trying to claw our way through the wardrobe into Narnia.

Paradoxically, playing fairies turned out, for our little gang, to be far more contentious than playing Cowboys and Indians. The three of us – Shelagh, a neighbour called Gloria and I – fought relentlessly for the key roles. We all, even Jim/Shelagh, desperately wanted to play Titania. This was not a gender issue. It had more to do with power and with the languid nature of the role. Titania lay around all day in her bower doing basically nothing, while the other fairies had to flit about providing lifestyle services for their queen.

'Bring me buttercups and wine!'

'Comb out my tresses, you worthless pixie!'

'Fashion me a neck pillow from yonder moss clump!'

Most of the time we were not competing for roles. Most of the time it all worked like a dream. Instinctively and without much discussion, we switched and swapped the tastes and proclivities normally associated with our respective genders. Shelagh was Robin Hood, and I was Maid Marian.

I was delighted to have a sister so ready and willing to pick up the slack in the butch department, and she was happy to butch it up. This symbiotic arrangement allowed our individual eccentricities and proclivities to blossom and intensify. Shelagh/Jim became very, very blokey, and I became more nelly with each passing year.

And everything was lovely.

And then it wasn't.

Being a year older, Shelagh went off to Caversham primary school, leaving me to while away another year of diarrhoea, violence and vomit at the orphanage.

Shelagh was assimilated without too many problems. Her tomboy persona was considered unremarkable. Lots of girls hated needlework and cookery and preferred to climb trees. Nobody questioned her Huckleberry Finn-ish ways. Nobody said, 'Hey, you up there in that oak tree. You needn't think we're going to stand idly by while you lay the foundation for a life of lesbianism. Get down here and finish your bloody needlework!'

Languishing in the mayhem of the orphanage, I had no idea what was in store for me. Sisterless, I whiled away the time learning to skip. No, I don't mean jumping-rope. I mean skipping as in skipping through fields of daisies. Skipping was good exercise and, given the considerable speed that was possible, enabled me to elude the insanity around me. But, most importantly, skipping felt extraordinarily pleasurable. The sensations of freedom, euphoria and speed acted like an antidepressant.

A year later I followed Shelagh to primary school and found out the horrid truth. While Shelagh's tomboy persona was a source of indifference, my nelly ways had the opposite effect. Everyone loves a tomboy, but an effeminate boy is reviled and doomed. Especially if he skips.

Don't fret. This is not going to turn into a gruesome sob story where I end up trying to hang myself with a pair of Betty's seamed nylons.

I saw what I needed to do. I formed a *salon des refusés*, comprising naughty girls and other girlie boys, like Biddie Biddlecombe. I ducked under the radar and found a way to survive.

And I learned to suppress the impulse to skip. This was a hard one for me, but somehow I managed it. I knew instinctively that learning *not* to skip was an important component of those legendary skills of conceal-ment which have enabled homosexuals to survive for centuries. These are, so they say, the same skills that have enabled so many limp wristers to become excellent government spies.

Chez moi, it was becoming apparent that I was not going to grow up to be like my tough Irish grandfather. Terry would throw a ball at me, and it would thud into my stom-ach. He did not make a big deal out of it. Nonetheless, I could not help noticing the look of disappointment.

Another Christmas was looming. What, in God's name, would I ask for? I could not go back to building aeroplanes. I decided to throw everyone off my scent.

'I simply must have a subscription to *Boy's Own Paper*,' I declared, thinking how ardent and masculine I must sound.

Terry's face lit up as if to say, 'Maybe you won't grow up to be an Eartha Kitt impersonator after all.' In Terry's defence, Miss Kitt was already looming large in my life. We now had a telly. Every week we watched *Sunday Night at the London Palladium,* a variety show on which leopard-clad Eartha was a frequent guest. I was barely able to contain my skippy enthusiasm for her outrageous purring performances.

Terry could not fill out that *Boy's Own Paper* subscription form quickly enough.

A month later, my very first issue popped through the letter box and thudded onto the carpet. With Oscar-winning enthusiasm, I tore it from its envelope and immersed myself in *boy culture.*

There are no words to describe the superhuman effort that it took for me to appear even remotely excited by this dreadful periodical. Each issue of *Boy's Own Paper* was more puritanically dreary and stultifyingly uninteresting than the last, especially the fiction. The *BOP* stories consisted of endless permutations of the Lassie theme: i.e. young boys prevailing in perilous situations with the help of devoted canines. Heaven forbid boys should have friends of either gender! These stories alternated with articles about repairing your own bicycle tyres, pet care and knot tying. With its unwavering commitment to the avoidance of anything remotely sassy or hedonistic, *Boy's Own Paper* was the magazine equivalent of a Taliban training camp.

I rehearsed a little speech: 'Dad, I must reluctantly bring to your attention the fact that *Boy's Own Paper* is lacking any editorial punch whatsoever. Besides, I now know all there is to know about tying knots, hamster care and how not to get struck by lightning, so I have decided I would rather have a subscription to *Vogue* instead.'

Who was I kidding? Cancelling the subscription was out of the question. This would have been a dead giveaway. The folks at *BOP* would have forwarded the information about my cancellation to the authorities, and I would have ended up on some international database for sissies.

And so, every month for years and years and years, the *Boy's Own Paper* plopped, turdlike, through our letter box, and everyone watched me pretend to care.

Eventually my self-imposed burka started to slip.

When I was twelve, and Betty asked me what I wanted for Christmas, I had half a mind to say, 'I want to park a truckload of explosives outside the offices of *Boy's Own Paper.*' But I didn't. Instead I dragged her to the local department store – the same store that would eventually employ me to flick a feather duster over the clocks and watches – pointed at the window, and declared, 'One of those!'

Strangely phallic but also wildly feminine, the object in question had haunted me for months. I would fabricate all kinds of reasons to pass by the store and stare at it. Standing about two feet high, this gorgeous object was made of red, hand-blown glass. The overall shape recalled the spire of a fantasy mosque from a camp Vincente Minnelli movie. The attenuated minaret was actually a removable stopper, suggesting that this object was some kind of decanter. But it was far too tall and unwieldy and insane to hold anything as pedestrian as sherry or olive oil. My decanter was fabulously and impudently non-functional. I did not know it at the time, but this gift was historic: it was my very first *decorative accessory.*

Betty seemed pleasantly surprised. Having grown up in an environment where überbutch Hellions and sociopaths were the male norm, she was no doubt intrigued and amused by my burgeoning aestheticism. Her comfort level about this purchase was much higher than mine.

I knew it was weird and that I was a freak and that only a pansy would want such a gift. But I couldn't help myself. Screw *Boy's Own Paper* and everything it stood for! This decorative accessory was completely and utterly *fabulous,* and soon it would be mine, all mine!

'I'm giving it to my son for Christmas. He picked it out himself!' said Betty with pride to the working-class saleslady with the auburn bouffant and the pursed lips.

The saleslady's eyes narrowed. 'Oooh! It's for 'im, is it?' she said with the air of one who would have liked to turn me over to the authorities and have me tried for crimes against humanity but instead decided she would torture and denounce me herself.

'How unuuuuuusual!' she shrieked with the obvious

intention of inciting a riot, 'I've never heard of a *boy* wanting something like thaaaat! What kind of lad are you?'

Shrivelling with embarrassment, I cast appeasing
glances at the rabble of passing shoppers. These were the
people who would soon be stoning me to death in the
gutter in front of the store while I clutched the broken
shards of my decanter and of my life.

Somehow we made it home without being discovered
or pillaged.

Safely ensconced in my room, I unwrapped the object
of my desire. All the shame and cringing subsided. With
one bold gesture, this fabulously useless object turned my
room into a groovy bachelor pad. I lay on my bed and
stared at it. I was in love . . . with a decorative accessory.

While I mooned over my decanter, my sister was undergo-
ing yet another gender reassignment. She was becoming
a girl.

Under pressure from her hormonally charged school
chums, Jim/Shelagh began wearing white lipstick and
hipster miniskirts. She switched hairdos, adopting the
Tom Jones, an insanely au courant 1960s style inspired by
the eponymous movie starring Albert Finney. The
creation of the Tom Jones involved a centre parting and
fringe. The hair was then ratted and tied back with a large
velvet bow at the nape of the neck. Flaunting her new
look, Shelagh started hanging out at the local bowling
alley and dating boys.

Soon she was consorting with a devastatingly handsome young man from the suburbs of Paris. Jean-Paul was a Vespa-riding romantic who swept her off her feet with bunches of daisies and whispered endearments. When she wasn't riding pillion with Jean-Paul, she was locked in her room listening to a 45 of 'Je T'Aime' the heavy-breathing hit song by Serge Gainsbourg and Jane Birkin.

She was no longer Jim. Her name had been concertinaed to Slag.

Like *mod* and *fab* and *dollybird*, the word *slag* was gaining popularity at the time. Not quite as harsh as the contemporary American *skank*, *slag* was nonetheless used to describe a dollybird of easy virtue. My sister, I hasten to add, was *not* a real bona fide *slag*: the Irish spelling of her name is to blame.

I applauded Slag's groovy, new Rive Gauche incarnation. Jean-Paul was *très beau*. If she could get a cute Frog boyfriend, then, by golly, so could I! But my love was the love that dared not speak its name. What to do? I resolved to while away the remainder of my teens living vicariously through my glam and increasingly Eurocentric sister.

Anything was better than living my own life, which was going from tragic to tragique.

If things at primary school had been less than fabulous, they now took a nosedive. Biddie and I were separated. He was sent to the school for clever kids. I was sent to the 'other school'. I felt pathetic and isolated. All I had was my decorative accessory, and even that was starting to depress me. Increasingly, that red decanter reminded me of my own freakishness. Nothing seemed to add sparkle to the vortex into which I was sliding. Not even the mysterious evaporation of *Boy's Own Paper*.

One day my mother came home from work and, as was her wont, poured herself a gigantic glass of Château Doonan. She then lit a Woodbine and began to cook dinner. While she cooked and smoked and drank, she regaled us with the highlights of her day at the BBC News Centre, where both she and Terry were now employed.

It was the usual hilarious stuff. Uneducated Betty was a good mimic with a wicked tongue who took great delight in skewering her college-educated colleagues and bosses. She was a natural raconteur who never seemed short of material. Adding to her overall charisma was the fact that she was an active, highly motivated union shop steward, happy to blow the whistle the minute she suspected her girls were overworked, overheated, or underventilated. Betty took great delight in agitating for improved working conditions and would recount, word for word, how she brought her bosses to heel.

On this particular occasion the self-congratulatory part of Betty's monologue went on a bit too long, and my attention started to wander. I began to flick through one of Betty's magazines in search of more titbits about the Beautiful People. Since reading about the Principessa

Pignatelli, I had become something of a Beautiful People watchdog. Seen through the glamour-crazed prism of my desperate gaze, every article and every ad seemed to refer either directly or indirectly to the Beautiful People. The adjectives that evoked them were *lithesome, radiant, international, jet-setting*. They seemed to me like a mysterious, all-knowing force from whom the rest of us could learn so very, very much.

Suddenly Betty switched topics and immediately recaptured my attention. While slicing Aunt Phyllis's food, she gave us the latest gossip from a colleague named Eve. Eve was a snappily dressed young lady who was married to a ballroom-dancing instructor. Unencumbered by children, Eve and hubby lived in a nice block of flats and enjoyed a relatively stylish, vomit-free existence. My ears always perked up when their names were mentioned.

According to Betty, a couple of very interesting men had moved into the flat above Eve. They were both bachelors. Always well dressed and meticulously groomed, these new arrivals had apparently christened their apartment with a wild, all-male champagne party. Eve knew it was champagne because she had heard the corks popping, and subsequent shrieks of delight, over the blare of Motown dance hits.

Betty referred to Eve's new neighbours as the Nancy Boys.

Over the course of the next few weeks, there followed a steady flow of anecdotes about the Nancy Boys.

One evening Betty informed us that the Nancy Boys had changed their habits. The rattle of cocktail shakers and the shrieks of Diana Ross had, much to the relief of Eve and hubby, been replaced by a strange, eerie silence. She knew the Nancy Boys were still in residence because, every so often, the stillness was broken by a disturbing repetitive noise.

Eve described it as a rhythmic, repetitive rasping, as if someone was walking on gravel. *Cheuw! Cheuw! Cheuw!*

At other times it sounded like a knife slicing a cabbage or the clearing of a smoky throat, but always very rhythmic and always quite loud, as if whatever was producing the noise was located directly on the floor.

Days went by, and the *Cheuw! Cheuw! Cheuw!* continued. Speculations about the origins of the noise reached lunatic heights. Eve was convinced that it was some kind of sexual thing. She based this on the fact that the rasping noise was occasionally punctuated by shrieks of appreciation, as in 'Oooooh, lovely!'

'Sounds satanic to me,' said Betty as she casually incinerated a tick from Hawo's furry forehead with the white-hot tip of her Woodbine. 'They are probably casting runes and drawing hexagons on the floor.' She warned Eve to watch her back and mind her own business.

A couple of weeks later, Betty held court once more, this time to a smaller audience than usual. The television was broken, which was no great loss, since Betty, post-supper, was always a great deal more amusing. There were just four of us at the dining room table: myself, Hawo the cat, Lassie and Aunt Phyllis. Terry was working nights. My sister, decked out in her tweed hipster mini and her Tom Jones bouffant had, somewhat scandalously, gone to the movies with a West Indian boy who lived down the street.

Uncle Ken was also dating. In a rashly optimistic moment, his doctor had told him he should find a woman and get married. Ken had promptly washed and shaved and headed out to the 'glee club' at the Huntley & Palmers biscuit factory. Here, on his very first foray as a swinging single, he met a rosy-cheeked, well-meaning Christian lady called Pat. They were now engaged.

Hawo, Lassie, Aunt Phyllis and I were, as usual, in my mother's thrall. Apart from being fascinated by Betty's witty repartee, I was desperate for an update on the Nancy Boys. I was much too inhibited to ask any direct questions. Instinctively I knew that by showing an interest in these men I would be giving away something strange and secret about myself.

Finally I plucked up the courage to ask. 'Is the *Cheuw! Cheuw! Cheuw!* still going on?'

Betty yawned. She plopped her bag of hair rollers on the dining room table and erected a small mirror, creating an impromptu dressing table.

'Oh yes, I forgot to mention it,' she said, winding a handful of bleached hair around a pink sponge roller. 'It's all back to normal. The *cheuw!* finally stopped.'

Betty paused to puff on her ciggie before grabbing another roller. 'And the Nancy Boys had another party last Saturday.'

I could not believe how nonchalantly she had withheld all this critical information! I was beside myself for more details. Betty was so annoyingly blasé about the whole thing. Chin in hands, I stared at her as if to say, 'I'm assuming this is the beginning of a very long and detailed account of said party.'

She rallied slightly. 'Eve said nothing much happened. As usual, it went on half the night. She watched from her balcony and saw more Nancy Boys falling into the rose bushes. One of them was carrying a crocodile handbag. It's past your bedtime.'

Reluctantly I headed upstairs. As I got to the first landing, I heard Betty yell, 'Oh, yes. Eve said that all the Nancy Boys were wearing caftans. It was a caftan party. It's a new thing.'

A caftan party! Oh . . . my . . . God!

Red-faced and palpitating, I rushed to my room, threw myself on the bed, and gazed at my decorative accessory.

A caftan party!

Waves of incomprehensible joy surged through my body as I imagined the glamour and fun that must surely have been experienced by all those caftan-wearing Nancy Boys. Instantly I understood the *Cheuw! Cheuw! Cheuw!* It was the noise of two men cutting out fabric with pinking shears and making caftans!

Betty and Phyllis and Hawo and Lassie would never have been able to figure this out. Nor did they care. They were not Nancy Boys. But I understood everything.

I was a Nancy Boy.

It is hard to fully express the massive significance of the caftan party. At the age of 14, and in one fell swoop, I understood who I could become, how I might live, and, most importantly, what I might wear.

Becoming a Nancy Boy was clearly within the scope of my abilities. I knew I had what it took. Unlike the Beautiful People, the Nancy Boys were tangible and accessible. A bunch of them lived only blocks away! My mind raced with a thousand thoughts and questions. Maybe these two species were somehow connected? After all, somebody had to design the principessa's frock and maintain her bouffant. Who better than a Nancy Boy?

I felt a surge of optimism about life. There was a light at the end of the tunnel . . . and it was on a dimmer . . . and there was a handsome man in a caftan who knew everything about mood lighting.

I began to skip once more.

Being marginal and different had been an increasing source of agony to me. Now, with the right magazines, the right decorative accessories, and a pair of pinking shears, I understood that my freakiness was a huge, raging advantage. Nancy Boys clearly had a lot more fun than non-Nancy Boys!

Uncle Ken would never wear a caftan, let alone sew

one. He was not a Nancy Boy, but I was, and happily so. I felt relief to have differentiated myself from Uncle Ken in such a fundamental way. Being gay distanced me from his insanity and misery and cat vomit. Gay or straight, I was still vulnerable to the spectre of hereditary madness, but at least, when the men in white coats came to get me, I would be well lit and wearing a caftan of my own making.

Uncle Ken married the lady from the Huntley & Palmers Glee Club.

I did not go to the ceremony. Betty and Terry had asked me if I wished to attend. I had visions of Narg screeching toward me and biting my neck like Vlad the Impaleress. I declined. Besides, I was busy performing an exorcism.

Ken had moved out, and I was taking over his room. My burgeoning Nancy Boy sensibility was too big for the box room in which I had spent most of my childhood. It would find full expression in Ken's former quarters. But first I had to scrub and scrape and remove the patina of nicotine and madness with which this room was liberally coated. While Ken and Pat were tying the knot, I was disinfecting skirting boards wearing Betty's orange rubber gloves.

Though curious about the wedding, I was more than happy to rely on my sister's account of the proceedings. According to Slag, the guests arrived by public transport at a church hall in the town centre. The bride and groom also arrived by town bus. This was not some wacky Carnaby Street gesture. They arrived by bus because they arrived by bus.

Afterwards guests repaired to a small, dusty hall, where apple juice was served in paper cups. Ritz crackers were served on paper plates. Every expense was spared. Clearly they should have hired a few Nancy Boys to inject the occasion with a bit of international savoir faire.

Jump-started by my caftan epiphany, I embarked on a gradual, increasingly flamboyant coming out involving hair dye, ear piercing, outré outfits, and Noël Cowardish affectations, such as using the word *wonderful* at every possible opportunity.

Betty: Here's some powder for your athlete's foot.

Me: Oh! You are *wonderful*! Thank you sooooo much!

I inflicted my gayness on my family day by day, sequin by sequin, *wonderful!* by *wonderful!* I never sat Betty and Terry down and had the *big conversation* with them. What was the point in having a big showdown when I could dress and behave exactly as I wanted? Betty and Terry – God love 'em! – always seemed mildly amused by my shenanigans. My parents' loopy relatives had given them both a stratospherically high tolerance for unconventional behaviour, of which I took full advantage.

Slag's route towards Lesbos was far longer and infinitely more nuanced.

One day my sister came home from the bowling alley looking horribly crestfallen.

'It's a bad scene. Is there a cup of tea on the go?' she said, yanking off her velvet Tom Jones ribbon and hurling it onto the Caravaggioesque mound of fruit which Betty kept on the sideboard because it was life-enhancing.

Almost overnight, Slag had an entirely new group of friends. While her former chums ratted their hair and wore gobs of mascara and white lipstick, the new ones were more existentialist. They wore dark clothes and combed their hair in long, centre-parted rats' tails à la Joan Baez.

Slag and her new sisters rarely gambolled outside. They locked themselves in her room and listened to Buffy Sainte-Marie and Bob Dylan. They spewed feminist dogma at anyone who would listen. The new Slag ceased to resonate with my inner Nancy Boy. I preferred the girlie Tom Jones years.

Betty was less than pleased that Slag had elected to let her hair hang limply to her shoulders and would have preferred an upswept style. She did, however, applaud the irate, opinionated aspect of the new Slag. Feisty, disgruntled rhetoric of any description appealed to her Northern Irish temperament.

The following year Slag left home for college and disappeared from my view into academia. Years passed. I disappeared into the world of fashion and window dressing. Slag and I lost track of each other's ideals and hairstyles. She disappeared further into academia, devoting years to the study of bizarre green worms and acquiring a Ph.D. in marine biology. I moved to America and got a Ph.D. in hedonism.

Fast-forward to 1986. I am living in a high-rise apartment building in New York, a great pad for a caftan party. The phone rings. It's Slag. I am slightly anxious. We rarely call each other. I brace myself for the possibility of bad news.

'Slag! How are you?'

'I have become a lesbian. And don't call me Slag anymore. It's a bit sexist, don't you think?'

Gulp.

'Congratulations!' I say with as much enthusiasm as I can muster.

I then barrage her with questions. I have to get to the bottom of her story. The call to lesbianism is, after all, not an invitation to a life of glamour and caftans. It is more about oatmeal, hiking boots and bum bags. Where is the payoff? While gay men are often fêted, lesbians continue to be regarded with suspicion. There seemed to be, to my gay male eyes, no dangling carrots to prompt a gal to plunge willy-nilly down that Well of Loneliness.*

Shelagh's answers to my frenzied questions formed a crazy collage.

---

*The Well of Loneliness (1928): a brave but suicide-inducing early lesbian novel by a lady named Radclyffe Hall, whose friends wore monocles and favoured bulldogs over poodles.

She blamed her slow emergence first and foremost on *The Killing of Sister George*. This grotesque 1968 lesbian movie, though undeniably hilarious, is not exactly sensitive in its handling of the subject. The lead character, George, is a stereotypical bossy, drunken dyke who wears thick tweeds. She intimidates her ultrafem girlfriend, named Childie, by making her eat her cigar butts and threatening to force her to drink all of her bathwater. Shelagh had seen this movie at a sensitive moment in her late teens: the histrionics of Childie and George had caused her to remain in Hetero Town.

Feminism and activism followed. In 1982 Shelagh participated in the historic peace demonstrations at Greenham Common.

'A revelation! Nine miles of women holding hands around a US army base,' recalled my sister of this emotionally charged counterculture *womyn's* moment.

Betty travelled to Greenham Common to check in on her only daughter. She arrived just in time to see Shelagh and her feminist friends lie down in the street in front of massive, revving trucks carrying the thrusting phallic Pershing missiles. (*Quel* irony!)

Though basically quite rightwing, Betty quickly entered into the spirit of things. She shared her cigarettes and some World War II stories with Shelagh's new chums. A wonderful day was had by all.

'OK, I understand the feminism and the Sapphic

camaraderie, but when and how did your interest in men evaporate?' I asked in the shrill tone of one who could not imagine losing his interest in men. Betty had kept me up to date on the steady string of boyfriends – a sheepdog trainer, a schoolteacher, a Lebanese pastry chef, a Jesuit priest – who had captured Shelagh's heart at various times in the intervening years. How and why had she given them all the heave-ho?

By this time my sister was getting slightly irritated.

'OK. It's really quite simple,' she barked, sounding quite tough and dykey and a tad like Sister George.

'Are you ready?'

'Yes!'

'You see! Women . . . actually talk to each other. Most straight men are not interested in having a decent two-way conversation!' said Shelagh with the relieved air of a woman who had just realised she would never be bored to death by a bombastic hetero male ever again.

I was about to challenge this idea. Then thought better of it. There was not a lot of point in trying to make sense of the mystical, magical realm of sexual identity. Shelagh was a lesbian and I was a poofter.

I remember well the last time my sister received a gift from Vivian and Marigold. It was a small mauve, enamelled powder compact. By this time Jim/Slag/Shelagh had long since stopped wearing make-up. I, meanwhile, had been experimenting with it for several years.

We asked Betty to intercede and let Marigold and Vivian off the hook.

'Call them up and tell them we're both gay. Do them a big favour!' said Shelagh, clipping on her bum bag in preparation for a morning constitutional.

Betty had a word with our kindly red-headed aunt, and the gifts stopped. When asked if she had mentioned our proclivities, Betty replied, 'No, of course not. Are these shoes too high for a woman my age?'

I guess it is not the easiest thing in the world to tell your in-laws – whose three children are all straight – that both your kids turned out queer. Nonetheless, my sister and I were disappointed. Betty had missed an opportunity to strike a blow for gay equality. (We were also terrified that, without sufficient deterrent, the gifts might start up again.)

I was determined to find out what our mother had actually said to Aunt Marigold. I waited until we were alone, and then I pursued the matter with her. Had she, for example, said something like 'Simon and Shelagh are both horribly ungrateful and don't deserve any gifts, so please stop *now*!'

Or maybe she'd been more creative: 'Marigold, I regret to inform you that they have joined a cult and are not allowed to have any possessions, so everything you give them is sold and goes to fund the needs of the cult.'

I had to know.

Betty lit a ciggie and glared at me. Mater did not like to be backed into a corner. A triumphant twinkle appeared in her eye, indicating that she was ready to respond, with confidence and verve, to my probing.

I braced myself.

'When I was in the air force,' she began, sounding not unlike her actress namesake, the Academy Award-winning Miss Davis, 'there were men in the cookhouse who plucked their eyebrows' – puff, pause, exhale – 'and they wore Max Factor midnight-blue eye shadow' – puff – 'and *I stuck up for them*!'

Pause. Puff.

'So don't you talk to me about gay rights. If you want someone to march in your parade, *I'm your man*!'

Chapter 9

VERMIN

THE FIRST time I got arrested I was wearing a Mickey Mouse printed shirt. The background was Easter yellow, and the Mickey Mouses were, as per usual, black and white with red and yellow clothing and accessories. The oversized collar of this shirt was cut with boldly rounded, cartoonish tips instead of points. It was purchased with trembling excitement from a trendy shop on Kensington Church Street called Mr Freedom, which specialised in garish, infantile-themed apparel for glam-rock devotees. There was a café adjacent to the store called Mr Feed'em.

I was embarrassingly proud of this purchase, funded as

it was by long hours of summer holiday toil at the Reading department store whose motto was 'Never knowingly undersold.'

'Wait till the girls get a load of this little number,' I mused as I carefully folded it in preparation for my return to Manchester University for the start of the autumn 1971 term.

The females in question – my college housemates – were named Angela, Joy and Rose. Angela was a pink-cheeked, brown-eyed cutie from the Isle of Man. Joy was a local girl with long, straight hair and high cheekbones whose celebrity lookalike might have been a young Judy Collins. Last but not least, there was Rose. This tall East Yorkshire brunette played the organ at the church in her tiny village. Rose was not quite as worldly as the rest of us, but she was catching up fast.

Together we rented a run-down terraced house in a part of Manchester called Whalley Range, pronounced 'Wolleh Rrrrrange' by the locals. The decor was visionary. Designed and furnished by our Pakistani landlord with random wall-papers and sticks of furniture from the Salvation Army, our house resembled a crack den a full fifteen years before the advent of crack.

The adjacent neighbourhoods were all in the process of being demolished. Everywhere you looked the sordid hovels of the Industrial Revolution, with their backyard toilets and smoking chimneys, were being levelled. This was all fine and dandy. However, anytime the wrecking balls started to swing, a river of displaced vermin surged out from under the rubble, down the street, and into our living room. Mice ran across our pillows while we slept. They scampered on top of the gas metre while watched by us from the safety of our scrungy couch.

It was an urban calamity of biblical proportions. If the bubonic plague had still been active, we would all have died.

We were ambivalent about our new friends. On the one hand, they were disgusting, never failing to leave a trail of horrid little turds wherever they went. On the other hand, they provided us with hours of light entertainment, something that, on our overly earnest college campus, was in short supply. University life had fallen short of our collective expectations. The year was 1971: there was no lack of countercultural rhetoric and radical ideals. But where was the glamour? Where was the fun?

It was around this time that Margaret Thatcher elected to eliminate the tradition of free school milk. This angered our fellow students far beyond our comprehension. Most came from upper-middle-class backgrounds. None of them had ever been at risk of calcium deficiency. Nevertheless, there were endless demonstrations at which Thatcher was vilified as if she were on a one-woman crusade to bring back rickets. The soundtrack to our college years consisted of thousands of raised students' voices shouting, 'Milk-snatcher Thatcher! Milk-snatcher Thatcher!'

Angela, Joy, Rose and I were significantly absent from the throng. We were pathetically apolitical. The girls and I were far more concerned with alcohol than with milk. We were, to put it bluntly, drunks. While our fellow students got high on pot, we drank ourselves stupid on beer and highly intoxicating Devonshire cider.

Having grown up in the Doonan winery, I had come to think of myself as a fairly experienced boozer. Then I met Angela, Joy and Rose, and immediately felt like a light-weight. Angela and Joy were seasoned drinkers, and Rose was making up for her church-playing years.

Joy, being a Manchester native, knew all the best bars. She loved to drag us all to a Dickensian, proletariat watering hole called Yates's Wine Lodge in the centre of town. Here we spent the evening ingesting lethal concoctions called 'blobs'. These hot, sugary, wine-based drinks tasted like cold remedies and, based on the frightening condition of the Yates' regulars, were guaranteed to rot both your teeth and your brain.

Like many pub habitués, Joy was a serious darts player. Her team even won the occasional tournament. Their winning strategy consisted of one part skill and nine parts blobs. It was amazing to watch Joy – fag in one hand, dart in the other – wobble and sway, throw a bullseye, and then collapse on the floor.

Angela, Joy and Rose were instant converts to Château Doonan. At the beginning of every term, I would transport as much of Terry's home-made wine to Manchester as I could carry on the train. The girls and I were so glad to see each other – and the free hooch – we would usually knock it all back in one evening.

Joy and I were probably the most enthusiastic imbibers. We medicated our anxiety with booze. In addition to sharing my obsession with the losing of one's marbles, Joy was terrified she would one day end up a bag lady. Any time she encountered a homeless person – there was no shortage in Whalley Range – she would shiver and reach for the cider.

One night Rose and Angela went out on the town with their men-friends, leaving Joy and me to our own devices. We spent the evening knocking back drinks, smoking furiously, talking incoherently, and listening to Lou Reed's album *Transformer* over and over again.

By 9.30pm we were already past the point of any restraint. Soon we had drunk everything in the house. There we were, slumped on the couch watching the mice running up the tattered curtains, with no money to go out and no more hooch on the premises.

Or was there?

With a sudden burst of optimistic energy, we both leapt off the couch and began searching every nook and cranny of the kitchen. Finding nothing but a half-empty bottle of vinegar only seemed to fuel that raging there-must-be-some-booze-somewhere conviction.

Like Jack Lemmon and Lee Remick in *Days of Wine and Roses,* we went into a ransacking frenzy.

After tearing through every room in the house, we eventually hit the jackpot. Lurking under Rose's dressing table was a bottle of Terry's wine. How sneaky of her to hide it there!

'Maybe Rose has one of those drinking problems. Whaddya callit?' slurred Joy unsympathetically as I glugged the entire contents of her stash into two pint-sized beer glasses we had recently stolen from the pub around the corner.

The rest of the evening is a bit of a blur. More Lou Reed. More incoherent but heartfelt babbling regarding our respective insecurities. I have a vague recollection of staggering across the street and unsuccessfully trying to get credit at the fish and chip shop.

I woke the next morning feeling very strange. My stomach ached, and my breath and clothes stank of witch hazel.

'Who used all my home-made rose-petal astringent? Were you having one of your evenings of beauty?' demanded Rose, as she waved the empty bottle accusingly in my blotchy face.

Joy and I should have expected as much. It was so very typical of Rose to be making her own beauty products.

Rose was very proto-Linda McCartney , but on a tight budget. Her insane brand of creative self-sufficiency knew no bounds. Rose was the kind of girl who, given a bit of encouragement, would have pulped and perforated her own toilet paper. Sunday mornings usually found her straining sour milk through an old pair of tights in a

valiant attempt to make her own cottage cheese. It was
hardly surprising that she made her own astringent.

What, you may well ask, had become of my quest to find
the Beautiful People? Well, in our own feckless way, we
were doing our level best. Joy, Angela, Rose and I were
trying hard to live a gracious and glamorous existence.

Though negligent on all aspects of house cleaning and
homemaking, we put a gargantuan amount of effort and
creativity into what the English call 'getting tarted up'.
We might not have been the Beautiful People, but we
were definitely the Tarted Up People, the Tarted Up
People of Whalley Range.

From the very moment we moved in together, we
turned our living room into a bustling atelier of haute
couture. Angela's bright-blue sewing machine was parked
permanently in the middle of the room. There were paper
patterns everywhere and a hissing iron on a permanently
erected ironing board.

The girls made mostly sassy blouses and party frocks,
and I made shirts for myself out of 'novelty' vintage
fabrics. When her boyfriend proposed to her, Angela ran
out, bought ten yards of cream crepe, and whipped up her
own wedding dress. For the next two weeks we all pinned
and primped around her like the Disney tweetie birds
in *Cinderella*.

We augmented our home-made garments with
secondhand finds acquired at church jumble sales. On

Saturdays, while our fellow students charged into the town centre for more anti-Thatcher demos, we headed in the opposite direction, to the suburban church halls.

There is nothing like the prospect of a good jumble sale to take your mind off a pounding hangover. Once inside we would hurl ourselves into piles of smelly and discarded clothing in search of vintage gems culled by church ladies from the houses of the Manchester bourgeoisie.

Occasionally I would find a hand-knit Fair Isle sweater or a Clarice Cliff teapot for myself, but most of my energy went towards ferreting out glamorous looks for the girls. Like a pimp who wanted his protégées to look extra-foxy, I trawled for bias-cut silk gowns, floral crêpe tea dresses, 1940s platforms, shoulder-padded Joan Crawford suits, exotic 1950s plate-shaped hats, and fox stoles.

For us Tarted Up People, fashion, and the wearing and flaunting thereof to pubs and discos, provided a nice anti-dote to dreary academic obligations. The girls and I were all psychology majors, and none of us was enjoying it very much. We were all horrified by the scientific rigour of our chosen subject. It was agonisingly boring. I vividly remember experiencing actual physical pain during our lectures.

None of us had read the prospectus very carefully before applying to Manchester University. We naïvely thought we would spend days interpreting each other's dreams and comparing Jung and Freud. I had additional expectations: I anticipated finding out why my family was insane and how to avoid a similar fate. Much to my annoyance, we hardly even touched on personality disorders, never mind mental illness.

We spent our days measuring and analysing instinctive behaviour as if it was a complicated disease like lupus. Human foibles were regarded with suspicion, so most of our studies centred on vermin. Instead of studying people, we studied rats – pretty white ones with pink eyes – and then we applied advanced statistics to our observations. Our team of all-male professors and teachers actively discouraged us from reading or discussing anything philosophical or amusing or insane or camp.

One day at a jumble sale Rose found a textbook on the origins of psychosis. A quirky, riveting tome like this would never have found its way onto one of our reading lists. It was much too interesting, and there were photographs! Of people. Mad people. This was more like it! We pored over it as if it were illicit pornography.

As I leafed excitedly through this book, I came upon a picture of a tubby, catatonic schizophrenic lady sitting on her bed with her head wreathed in tea towels.

'How you is she? You're always doing that!' said Angela with a chuckle, sending a chill of panic down my spine.

Instantly I had a raging anxiety attack.

Angela was right. I had developed an unconscious habit, while lounging *chez nous*, of wrapping stuff, like towels and scarves and even cushions, round my head. Even in warm weather.

Rose's book said that people went bonkers in their late teens or early 20s. Maybe my one-way ticket to Narg-ville had finally arrived, but with a difference. I had never before considered the possibility that I might become a catatonic schizophrenic. I had always thought that, when I eventually went gaga, I would be upholding the fine family tradition of paranoid schizophrenia.

My anxieties quadrupled when I found out that our entire psychology class was scheduled to make a field trip to a mental hospital.

'What the hell's wrong with you?' asked Angela as she stitched a new frock for the occasion. 'Finally we're going to study people instead of bloody rats!' But I was suspicious. The trip was very unexpected and clearly at odds with our curriculum. Maybe they were planning to drop me off.

I attempted to defray my anxiety by getting tarted up. I donned a pair of extra-wide Oxford bags, a navy and white satin jockey jacket (home-made and copied from a Mr Freedom design) and ladies' cartoonish sandals. These shoes were styled like kiddies' footwear but sized up and fabricated in metallic blue leather. Very Elton John.

The lunatic asylum was everything I might have imagined. The grim Victorian Gothic façade soared ominously against the leaden sky. Narg-like women cowered under wind-blown trees, while Ken-like men and their uniformed attendants shuffled along tarmac paths looking like something out of *Night of the Living Dead*. Angela, Joy, Rose and I started eyeballing the more attractive males.

Our professor then broke the news that we had not come to hobnob with the inmates. Our destination was a clinic where doctors treated their patients with *aversive conditioning*. We had been studying the effects of aversive conditioning on rats. Would they still go for the food pellet even if they got an electric shock? Etc, etc, etc.

The girls and I had also been studying the effects of aversive conditioning at home on our own rodents. We allowed them to nibble at morsels of Rose's cheese and then whacked them with a jumble sale badminton racket. Many of them seemed willing to brave the badminton racket for the possibility of a nibble of Rose's cheese, a testament to the flavour and quality of her dairy products if nothing else.

'We treat everything from phobias to homosexuality,' announced the doctor once we were inside the grim Orwellian clinic, causing me to wince slightly. We were then shown slides of bare-chested California surfer types with tousled locks. I instantly fell in love. Not only were they beautiful and tanned but they seemed so shockingly carefree and happy, happy, happy.

Not wishing to appear sleazy, I redirected my gaze. There, illuminated by the glow of the slide show, were the chairs into which the patients were strapped while electricity was applied to their various parts. It was all very *Clockwork Orange*.

I couldn't help wondering why any gay personage would opt to come to a grim loony bin and submit to this kind of torture, as opposed to, for example, going to one of the fab local discos, drinking a lot, and then picking up a hairdresser or even an insurance salesman.

Since moving to Manchester, I had achieved some modest success in the dating department. Upon first arriving, I met a part-time circus acrobat who sold bags of Dolly Mixtures off a barrow in the open-air market for extra cash. It did not amount to anything, but I took it as proof positive that there were pleasant, interesting young men to be dated. One just had to be patient. The life of a poofter, though not without its emotional whoopee cushions and discriminatory aspects, was certainly not dire enough to throw in the towel and get yourself electrocuted.

The doctor explained that it was not possible to embark upon a course of aversive conditioning without first identifying the criteria for successful treatment. Without these benchmarks it was impossible to tell if the electric shocks were working.

'For example,' said the doctor again, focusing his spiel in my direction, 'in order to cure a man of his impulse to wear ladies' garments, it is first necessary to identify a series of behaviours and designate them as either feminine or masculine.'

Angela and I started nudging each other. I giggled nervously.

The doctor continued in his hauntingly flat monotone. 'At one end of the spectrum would be such things as wearing lipstick, at the other, smoking a pipe or growing a moustache.'

Dr Strangelove continued, 'The transvestite who desires to be "cured" is shown pictures of himself dressed as a lady and simultaneously given electric shocks. The success or failure of the treatment is measured by tabulating changes in the number of subsequent masculine and feminine behaviours.'

By this point I was starting to feel a bit indignant. Why would any self-respecting cross-dresser subject himself to this ridiculous ordeal? And why was Dr Strangelove torturing these poor souls instead of encouraging them to simply throw on a frock and join the other bespangled trannies down at the Picador, a local club owned by the outrageous Foo-Foo Lamar.*

The evil doctor admitted that the treatment, because it was dealing with the foibles and complexities of human beings, was not perfect. (Subtext – you losers should just stick to studying rats and mice because people are simply too weird.)

'Establishing criteria in these areas of human behaviour is an innately flawed process,' he continued.

---

*Foo-Foo was a very well-known, nightclub-owning drag performer who happened to live next door to Joy's mum. When, years later, Foo-Foo died, the whole city, including football stars like David Beckham, turned out. Manchester has always loved a trannie.

The cross-dressers' criteria, in particular, were apparently fraught with problems. 'We have found that there are very few behaviours that are either exclusively male or exclusively female. There are normal, healthy women who smoke pipes, and there are fully functional males who dye their hair or even curl their eyelashes.'

The room went very quiet. At this point not just the doctor but the entire class seemed to be staring at me.

He went on. 'There is, however, one activity that is completely and utterly exclusively female and which normal, healthy men never ever, ever, ever do,' boomed the glaring doctor. 'I am referring to *the painting of the toenails*.'

With a curt 'good day!' the doctor concluded his talk, banged on the overhead fluorescent lights, and swept out, leaving the entire class staring in the direction of my trendy sandals.

Now, with the lights back on, everyone could see the metallic red glow through the perforations over my toes. Yes, I had broken the last taboo. I had painted my toenails.

Angela and Rose had painted their toenails too. We were all beautifying ourselves in preparation not for the loony bin but for a much-anticipated end-of-term jaunt to nearby Blackpool. The bottle of polish had been sitting on the coffee table on Rose's psychosis manual for an entire week. It was just too tempting.

At this point, our tour disintegrated into a German Expressionist nightmare. The whole class hooted at me, pointing and screaming with laughter. I could not get out of that loony bin fast enough.

After a few vats of cider, the feelings of embarrassment began to recede. It was actually quite nice to be the centre of attention.

A week later our train arrived in Blackpool. The sea front was packed with loud-mouthed day trippers who scarfed down whelks and guzzled beer and wore hats that said 'Kiss me quick'. They were all terribly common.

And so were we. Thanks to a couple of flagons of Devonshire's finest consumed on the train, Angela, her boyfriend, Rose and I were feeling excitable, happy and quite plastered. Joy was not with us: she had stayed in Manchester for an important darts tournament.

Lubricated by more booze, we could not help but enter into the spirit of things, enjoying the rides and braying at ourselves in the distorting mirrors. It wasn't long before we got that ravenous I-could-eat-a-whole-box-of-cereal hunger which afflicts excessive drinkers.

Ducking into a greasy café, we nervously eyed the menu. I realised that I had never dined out with my girls. We spent all our university grant money at either the pub or the fabric store.

During my childhood we rarely dined in restaurants. Betty and Terry had neither the cash nor the inclination to eat out, which was just as well, since the choices were limited to say the least. Once a year, on Betty's birthday, we went to a Chinese place in the high street called the Tai Kwong. I remember it vividly because of the big painted sign on the window which read: WE DO ALSO TAKE AWAY HOT MEALS. The iffy grammar of this message kept us all in stitches, much to the embarrassment of the proprietor. My blind aunt Phyllis would make me read the sign over and over, changing the emphasis with each reading. We do *also* take away hot meals. We do also take *away* hot meals. Ha! Ha!

Back to Blackpool.

A large blonde waitress loomed over our table. I ordered beans on toast, as did Rose. We were anxious about the cost, and this was the cheapest thing on the menu. Devil-may-care Angela and her beau went berserk, ordering fried eggs, sausages, fried bread and something that was known in such establishments as 'scrape'.

'Scrape' was the accumulated, lard-infused, crunchy material that coagulates in the frying pan during the course of cooking other items, such as bacon or sausages. Scrape was collected and then, somewhat brazenly and disgustingly, sold to delighted patrons as an artery-clogging side dish. Nobody could ever accuse the English of lacking an understanding of *the finer things of life*.

We ate hungrily. The bill arrived. We stared at it.

I cannot recall who suggested that we run out of the restaurant without paying. Angela always maintained it was me. I still maintain it was her. One thing is for sure, there was no voice of moderation saying, 'This is a really cheap meal. Why don't we just pay for it?' We lacked that kind of leadership.

A collective panic infected us. Once the notion of flight had been posited, all conversation stopped. We stared at each other furtively, waiting to see who would make the first move. We could not go back. There was a ridiculous inevitability to the whole thing. Nobody wanted to be left holding the bill for all that delicious fare, and yet nobody wanted to be labelled the instigator of a potentially nasty incident.

Then it happened. In jittery unison, we all rose.

Accelerating wildly, we bolted, as one, out of the greasy café and into the sunlight.

The scrape eaters dived into Boots the Chemist. Rose headed for Woolworth's. And I, for reasons I have never been able to identify, went barrelling towards the beach.

Down on the sand, the working classes of the North of England stared at me in an unfriendly way, as if I was unwanted street theatre or possibly a lunatic. As I charged through their midst, kicking sand hither and thither, they clutched their cardigans about them and held their children close. Some even hurled obscenities. What was wrong with them? Hadn't they ever seen a man in a Mickey Mouse shirt, high-waisted, navy-blue, pleated Oxford bag trousers, and matching navy-blue, women's Bata platform ankle boots with four-and-a-half-inch heels, teetering across the sand before?

I loved the platform shoe era. In my Bata boots I went from five feet, four and half inches to five nine, and it felt great. Don't get me wrong, I wasn't neurotic about my lack of height. When I was 13, I was the tallest kid in the class. Then I stopped growing. I never grew another inch. But I wasn't bitter. Height seemed like a biblical kind of concept. It was something that could be given and then taken away again. One had to just roll with it and wait it out. Sure enough, when the 70s arrived, platforms returned and I was tallish again.

As I – all five feet nine of me – dashed through the pale holidaymakers in my groovy Kensington High Street look, it dawned on me that I might be rather easy to spot. *Conspicuous* was the word that sprang to mind. My suspicions were confirmed when suddenly, in the distance, I heard the shriek of our blonde waitress in hot pursuit. She had spotted me with the aid of a pair of World War II binoculars, which now hung around her neck, giving her an air of military efficiency. They were no doubt kept under the counter of the café for the purpose of hunting down flitting non-payers.

I am always impressed when chunky people, especially people whose arteries are clogged with years of scrape, turn out to be athletic. The strapping waitress rhinocerosed across the sand like a freight train, gaining on me rapidly. This was obviously not the first time she had been obliged to go the extra mile in order to get tipped.

Gradually her shrieks became louder. She was running about twice as fast as I was. In my defence, I was considerably handicapped by my footwear, the heels of which sank into the sand with each stride.

'Ay, you! Ya bastud! Stop runnin, will ya!' she yelled as she closed in on her prey, binoculars bouncing on her bosom. She was utterly terrifying.

I knew when I was licked. I stopped running and reached into my pocket. Even though I had had only beans on toast and no scrape, I was resigned to the idea that I would have to settle the entire bill. I prepared myself to charm and mollify the young lady. How hard could it be? Waitresses in greasy cafés were invariably attention-starved. I would compliment her on her athleticism and personal style. She was sure to see the humour in the whole escapade. I would give her our address in Manchester. 'If ever you're in Whalley Range, do drop by for some cottage cheese and home-made astringent!'

It did not quite work out like that. As my pursuer closed in on me, I saw with alarm that her feet were leaving the ground. There would be no charming, cheeky badinage. There would be no forgiveness. She hurled herself towards me. She was screaming like a martial arts demon.

We both fell in a sandy heap. She landed on top of me, clunking me on the head with those accursed binoculars. As we struggled to our feet, I realised, not without concern, that she had my right arm in a half nelson, again expertly administered from years of practice.

'Yoooer kummin wi me!' she said, looking abominably self-satisfied. Now came her moment of triumph as she strong-armed me back to the café in front of a sea of amused and applauding spectators. I don't blame them. As street theatre goes – and it usually doesn't – this was exceptionally entertaining stuff.

As we trudged towards the crime scene, I saw a police car parked outside the café. Leaning against it was a portly, red-faced, very un-glam-rock police officer.

'Is the circus in town?' he sneered, referring, I am assuming, to my imaginative attire. Anxiously, I pulled out my crumpled wad of money and, with a blizzard of heartfelt apologies, paid the bill.

But this wasn't enough for my uniformed friend. Before you could say 'Prisoner of Cell Block H', I was bundled into the back of his vehicle.

'Get in, Mary Poppins!' he said with a menacing snarl.

'How kind of you to drive me to the train station,' I said. 'But I'm quite happy to walk.' The policeman squealed off down the street with me in the passenger seat.

'I'm sure you must be terribly busy. Now why don't I just – '

'We're going to keep driving until we find 'em. All of 'em. Vermin like you aren't welcome in Blackpool!'

'Nor should we be, but I – '

'Is that them?' said the policeman gruffly, pointing at a group of senior citizens.

'No, my friends don't wear plastic rain hoods.'

'Is that them?' he said, pointing to a group of delinquents who were throwing balled up fish and chip wrappers at each other. He was determined that I should rat out my accomplices. And so was I. How dare they abandon me and leave me holding the scrape tab?

We drove around for almost an hour.

We ran out of things to say.

'You're nothing but a big girl's blouse,' said the policeman, using one of the more colourful North English colloquialisms assigned to people such as myself.

Eventually we both got bored. When we neared the railway station, he pulled over and dumped me on the pavement. 'Now fuck off back to Manchester, and if you ever come back to Blackpool I'll lock you up, and you know what happens to people like you in there . . . eh?'

'Thanks awfully, Officer,' I gushed and clomped off into the station, where I found my co-conspirators crowing triumphantly in the bar. Nobody was very interested in my tale of woe and public humiliation. They seemed to regard the whole escapade as some kind of hugely successful, fabulously executed heist.

I have never been back to Blackpool. These days I have to watch my cholesterol, and scrape is a big, fat no-no.

Chapter 10

DAUGHTERS!

I WAS BEING treated for a lisp, and Biddie was there because he dropped all his *t*s and *h*s.

In the late 1950s, Biddie and I found ourselves attending speech therapy classes, courtesy of Her Majesty's Government. We must have been about seven or eight years old.

It was all very Eliza Doolittle: Biddie had to repeat words like *bottle* and *house*, and I was forced to repeat more interesting phrases, like 'hot toast' and 'I swallowed a sackful of snakes'.

For some reason we also had to say 'Peggy Babcock'

over and over at high velocity: 'Peggy Babcock! Peggy Babcock! PEGGY BABCOCK!' This is a skill I have retained to this very day. Though I still cannot swallow a sackful of snakes without a lisp lapse, I can repeat the name Peggy Babcock with machine-gun efficiency and speed.

Viewed from the vantage point of the 21st century, these efforts at self-improvement probably seem embarrassingly bourgeois. I would ask the reader not to judge too harshly, and to remember that our Peggy Babcocks took place at a time when upwards aspiration was assumed, applauded and actively encouraged. Improved speech was the gateway to a middle-class life and all the benefits that came along with it.

It had not yet become cool to be common.

These poignant attempts at social betterment were by no means limited to me and Biddie and our state-sponsored speech therapy classes. All over the United Kingdom people were trying anything and everything to divest themselves of their regional working-class accents. The crisp, clear, modulated speech of radio and TV announcers was the ideal to which we all aspired.

The arrival of the telephone in British homes increased the pressure to 'act posh'. Phone users adopted what was known as a 'telephone voice'. Once a caller had been identified, it was customary to say, 'Air. Hair. Lair.' (translation: Oh hello!).

Not everyone wanted to play the game. There was a small number of very naughty people who aspired down instead of up: there were middle-class girls who drank too much sherry and got pregnant, and public school-educated aristocrats who splurged their family fortunes on drugs and dockyard prostitutes. Those who demonstrated these kinds of self-destructive behaviours were the objects of grave concern. They were going against the grain. They were ruining things for the rest of us. Anyone who was aspiring down instead of up ran the risk of being institutionalised and overseen by tight-lipped, pasty-faced nuns.

Biddie and I had no incentive to pretend to be more common than we already were. It made no sense whatsoever. We were determined to become more posh than we were, regardless of how many Peggy Babcocks it took to get there.

Fast-forward ten years.

The class struggle continues.

During my years at university, I attempted, fairly unsuccessfully, to craft a gay identity. It was hard to find a reasonable point of entry, if you'll pardon the expression. There seemed to be only two alternatives, both of which were quite extreme.

First there was the middle-class campus Gay-Lib Society. The hippies who dominated this scene had long hair and crushed velvet maxi-waistcoats. They were radical fairies. They sat on each other's laps at Gay-Lib meetings while knitting extra-long rainbow-coloured scarves; they scribbled poetry about wizards and magical pixies. These

Pre-Raphaelite nellies alternated between reading aloud from *The Lord of the Rings* and venting heartfelt homilies about repression. It was hard to take all the politicised babbling seriously, especially when everyone at these meetings was dressed up like Jethro Tull's big sister.

Luckily, there was an alternative.

The other option was, in its own way, even more exotic than the radical fairy culture. I'm referring to the local gay working-class pubs and clubs.

The indigenous Manchester homosexuals who drank in these dives were so waspishly feminine and catty they made the campus wizards look like Burt Reynolds. It was not their clothing: the working-class blokes were often dressed quite conservatively. It was their speech.

When I first walked into a pub and came upon this phenomenon, I felt like Margaret Mead stumbling upon a cache of albino pygmies.

It took me a moment to figure out what was going on.

As I stood at the bar, all I could hear were the words 'Daughter!' and 'Mother!' screeched over and over again. This was the sound of exuberant friends and acquaintances greeting each other at the end of the grim workweek. 'Mother!' 'Daughter!' 'Daughter!' 'Mother!' The practitioners seemed to derive immense pleasure from this activity. It was as if they were working through some horrible Oedipal trauma.

Gradually things became clearer. A social structure emerged.

These flamboyant men were divisible into two distinct groups: *mothers* and *daughters*. A *mother* was an older gay man who had a bit more money and more experience than the typical *daughter*. The *daughters* were the noisy rapscallions who cadged drinks and coquettishly teased the *mothers* about their age and their vanished looks.

I was fascinated and delighted. Having grown up in a house full of misfits and lunatics, I was always happy to stumble upon anything that made me feel less strange. But I needed someone into whose forearm I could dig my fingernails. I needed a witness to this pantomime of perversity.

The next day I wrote a letter to Biddie (one didn't phone in those days) and insisted that he visit Manchester for the weekend to experience the hilarious world of *mothers* and *daughters* for himself.

Two weeks later I met him at the train station. He looked amazing. With the help of one of his old girlfriends – he had gone through a straight phase, which coincided with an LSD phase – he had cobbled together a new glam-rock outfit. This consisted of a high-collared, home-made, sequined Roxy Music jacket, velvet knickers, silver space boots and a tangerine feather boa. His bright red Bowie hair shook like a nylon feather duster. The high collar of the jacket hid the gentle flow of blood that was coursing down his neck, the result of an aborted attempt to pierce his ear on the train with one of his grandmother's chandelier earrings. He was wearing false eyelashes and metallic copper eye shadow.

Fearing a less than warm reception from the gangs of Manchester United football supporters who roamed the station, I immediately dragged Biddie, suitcase in hand, straight to a pub called The Rembrandt. We ensconced ourselves at the bar just in time to watch the cabaret act. Two fire-eating drag queens in cheap beaded tops jumped through a Mylar curtain onto the card-table-sized stage.

The performers took turns swigging gasoline from a milk bottle and singeing their lips and hair. As we marvelled at this spectacle, we began to tune in to the adjacent conversations.

All around us men were *mothering* and *daughtering* each other relentlessly.

''Ere, daughter! Buy yer old mother a drink, would ya?'

'Daughter! Where have you beeeeen?'

'Who made yer outfit, daughter? Ya look 'orrible!'

'Oh! Mother! What *have* ya done to yer 'air?'

We began to study the nuances. The appellation *daughter,* from what we could tell, seemed a lot more common than *mother. Daughter* also seemed more palsy-walsy than *mother.* There were, however, exceptions. In addition to indicating friendship, *daughter* could be used as a brutal put-down, i.e. I'm calling you *daughter* even though we are the same age because I'm superior to you. Conversely, *mother* could be hurled at a fellow *daughter* to communicate the idea that, even though we are the same age, I am going to pretend that you are older than I am and that you are less attractive and should therefore buy me a drink. There were a million permutations. It was all about tone and intent.

If you wanted to be exceptionally evil, you could tease a really old homosexual about his age by, preposterously, calling him *daughter*, as in, 'Having a nice evening are you, daughter? A bit late for you, isn't it? Mind your step now.' This could also be done in a friendly way to remind an old *mother* of the days when she had once been a young and attractive *daughter*.

Biddie and I were in heaven. Here were fellow human beings who were actually more common and bizarre than we could have ever hoped to be. We spent the entire weekend inhaling the gloriously fetid atmosphere of this tawdry working-class microculture. In no time we were *daughtering* each other with skill and vehemence. Vehemence was important: every *'Daughter!'* had to be hurled as with a slingshot. Every *'Daughter!'* had her very own exclamation mark.

The highlight of the weekend came right before Biddie caught the milk train back to Reading. We stopped into The Rembrandt to catch the Sunday night cabaret.

The featured artiste was an ancient, one-legged crossdresser, who billed herself simply as MOTHER. GRANDMOTHER would probably have been more accurate. Having lost her leg in World War II, the ancient MOTHER was proud of her prosthetic limb and flaunted its flesh-coloured plasticity in a glittery minidress.

MOTHER's 'act' was even more heart-stopping than her appearance. She stood, arms and leg akimbo, on the little stage, drenched by a moody blue spotlight. Then, without any musical accompaniment, she delivered a deadpan recitation of Alfred, Lord Tennyson's 'The Charge of the Light Brigade'. All six stanzas of it. The choice of material prompted several unkind *daughters* to posit the theory that MOTHER had actually lost her leg in the Crimean War.

Biddie and I were transfixed by this Dada performance. The recitation was made all the more surreal by the fact that the *mothers* and *daughters* present ignored the entire thing. They caroused and screeched and smoked all the way through it, barely acknowledging MOTHER as she rode 'into the valley of Death'.

At the end of this weekend, we were both tired and happy and completely and utterly in the thrall of the *mothers* and *daughters* of the greater Manchester area. We had found a place where all the marginalised freaks of the world were welcome. Even us. We embraced our *daughterdom* with manic enthusiasm.

'Bon voyage, daughter!' I yelled as Biddie boarded the train home.

We were henceforth incapable of holding a conversation without *daughtering* each other to death. In no time we had lost our grip on parody and become bona fide *daughters*.

~

Fast-forward 30 years.

I'm living on another continent in another century.

My husband, Jonathan, has a solemn look on his face. He has something important to tell me. I am concerned. We are, as far as I am aware, very much in love and almost obscenely compatible. Here in New York, where griping about one's significant other is a daily pastime, our happy union is something of an anomaly. Is our relationship about to disintegrate? Am I about to enact one of those horrible scenes when a cataclysmic announcement is made and everything goes from blissful to nasty? Is he dumping me for somebody younger? Has he made arrangements to drop me off at a retirement home on our upcoming trip to Florida? My 50th birthday has just passed. Should I, like so many of my contemporaries, have zipped off to Brazil to avail myself of a cut-price liposuction–cosmetic surgery Xmas combo package? Has Jonathan become a Kabbalah devotee?

In measured tones, Jonathan lays out a new and revolutionary scenario for our lives. He tells me that he has decided to add to our ménage. Nothing kinky. Quite wholesome, in fact. He wants to hire someone who can cook our food and make our beds and fold his Lacoste shirts and arrange them by colour so they look like the ones in the store. He wants us to hire a live-in housekeeper!

'A housekeeper!' I shriek, clutching the area where pearls would be if I wore them. 'That's so insanely bourgeois! I have my image to think of. . .'

'You're middle-aged and you wear Gucci silk pocket squares,' says Jonathan in a kind and caring tone. 'No offense, but you have about as much street cred as Liberace.'

Fast-forward one hour.

Jonathan is out for the evening. I sally forth to rent something radical from the video store which will bolster my dwindling sense of street cred. This looks perfect: *Murder at the Gallop,* starring Margaret Rutherford as Miss Marple.

I order my take-out food and pop in the VHS tape.

Bicycling furiously, cape flying, Miss Marple returns home to her tiny thatched cottage after a hard day of sleuthing. She dismounts. With the air of a woman who would love nothing more than to take off her hot tweed outer garment, roll down her knee-highs, and make herself a fortifying cup of tea, she waddles towards her rustic, knotty front door.

Magically, the door opens. A uniformed housekeeper greets her, curtsies ever so slightly, and wooshes that cape from her shoulders. Miss Marple flops into a squishy old chair and, with forefinger and thumb, begins to rub her jowls in a meditative fashion, pondering her latest investigative conundrum. Within seconds the housekeeper returns, carrying a magnificent tea tray groaning with cucumber sandwiches and fresh-baked scones.

Street cred, schmeet cred! I'm sold.

~

Fast-forward one week.

Marita is from the Philippines. She is skinny and petite. She has the shoulder-length, pin-straight hair for which every woman in New York City would kill. The agency has sent only one applicant: Marita. We like her hair and her cheeky personality and hire her on the spot.

She moves into our spare room.

Upon learning of Marita, none of my friends and colleagues seems remotely concerned about my loss of street cred. They are infinitely more focused on our collective loss of privacy. When confronted with their horrified reaction, Jonny and I realise that we are both antiprivacy. We like togetherness. Privacy is a greatly overrated condition. If people have privacy, they start to do unsavoury things like surfing ghastly sites on the Internet, wearing preposterous undergarments, and berating one another in an uninhibited fashion. We have no doubt that Marita will have a moderating influence on our behaviour and our language, which can, without scrutiny, become appallingly obscene and provocatively un-PC within a matter of minutes.

Marita's first day. She has a question. She is unsure how to address us. Should she call us 'Mr Simon'? 'Mister Adler'?

I try to remember how Miss Marple's trusty aid addressed her. *Ma'am* is a tad frumpy. We decide to sleep on it.

Fast-forward 24 hours.

The smell of fresh-baked scones is wafting through the kitchen.

'I decide what I call you!' says Marita with a sparkle in her lovely blackcurrant eyes. 'You are like my mother, so I call you Mother. It's okay?'

'I don't see why not,' I reply, trying not to betray the fact that I am quite taken aback. Marita, as far as I know, has never even heard of Manchester.

'Yes, you may call me Mother if that is what you would like.'

'What about me?' says Jonny, sounding quite left out.

'You are like my daughter. So I call you Daughter!'

Mother and Daughter!

'And what about you? What shall we call you?' I ask, with the growing sense that this could be getting a little creepy.

'Mother, Daughter, you call me Nanny, because I am your nanny.'

Nanny, Mother, and Daughter!

We seal the deal with a group hug.

The best thing about having Nanny in our home is not the cooking or the cleaning. The best thing is watching people's concerned expressions when, at social gatherings and family functions, our nanny uninhibitedly calls out, 'Mother! Daughter! You want me to serve food now?'

Chapter 11

PUDDING

BIDDIE and the oversized floor pillow and Happy
Harry and I eventually got sick of sharing one room.

We moved to a larger pad in a cheaper area. The
kitchen and bathroom were still down the hall, but at
least we could go about our daily business without having
to kick the floor pillow out of the way.

Our pad was drearily unmemorable, with the exception of a startlingly white vinyl floor, which ran through-
out. Though disastrous from an acoustic point of view –
especially when Biddie was rehearsing his new cabaret act
– this spanking new floor covering gave the place a crisp,

optimistic look and provided a contrasting background which showed off the floor pillow to full advantage. This white floor plays a significant role in the incident I am about to relate.

Our street was called Leamington Gardens, which sounds very EM Forster but wasn't. Admittedly there were no tarts in our building. But there was definitely one across the street.

She was a large, attractive, very lazy, very unusual Jamaican lady. She did not trudge the streets braving the elements like a regular tart. Nor did she make any effort to adorn herself in a profession-appropriate manner, with the usual sequinned frocks or spangled eyelids. She was never to be seen flaunting herself at closing time under the lamplight outside the neighbouring pubs.

Jamaican Lady preferred to solicit her clients from the comfort of her front porch. Here she stood for hours at a time, looking detached and vacant and slightly haunting. This was unusual behaviour for a British tart. London streetwalkers in particular have always been known for their cheeky verbosity, enticing potential clients by calling out phrases such as 'How about a night of fun, dearie?' or the simpler 'How about it?'

Not Jamaican Lady. She was mute and uninviting. Her torpid body language seemed to say, 'How about a night of unrelieved tedium?'

When it came time to advertise her services, she did so with one simple gesture. She lifted her skirt.

Jamaican Lady rarely even blinked or coughed. She seemed very focused on conserving her energy, limiting her actions strictly to the aforementioned lifting of the aforementioned skirt. She did not even bother to lower her skirt manually. She would simply release it and allow gravity to do the work. It was as if she thought that any physical exertion would burn calories, which in turn would diminish her figure, which even to a homosexual window dresser, seemed to be remarkably voluptuous.

The neighbourhood was not entirely without its classy interludes. Two young professional classical singers lived on the third floor of our house. They were boyfriends. One was a gifted counter-tenor who specialised in ancient castrati choral numbers. He sang, much to our undisguised fascination, in a staggeringly impressive prepubescent choirboy trill. His singing was miraculously effortless, a pair of lightly flushed cheeks being the only sign of exertion.

His speaking voice, when he came down to borrow a cup of sugar or ask us to stop screeching, was quite normal. But whenever he sang, out would pour this high-pitched river of gorgeous Renaissance song. We would ply him with cheap wine and then beg him to perform and then gawk at him as if he was some kind of freak, which of course he was, in a high culture kind of way.

His chum, by contrast, was a booming bass with an improbably deep Paul Robeson voice. When he sang, he frowned continuously and made intimidating gestures with his large, murderous hands while his adoring husband looked on.

These talented young songbirds – we nicknamed them Boris and Doris – would practice individually for hours. More often than not they would punctuate their rehearsals with a corny duet. To the passers-by, even Jamaican Lady, their singing must have conjured up a cliché romantic coupling. Nelson Eddy and Jeanette MacDonald. Nobody on the block had any idea that they were listening to two blokes.

Boris and Doris were at opposite ends of the scale, yin and yang. It was tempting to make hasty assumptions about their private lives. 'It's easy to see who wears the pants and who wears the earrings,' cackled Biddie as soon as they were out of earshot, whereupon we winked and nudged each other like two smug fishwives.

Biddie's observations turned out to be an oversimplification. Just when we thought we had them figured out, they moved the gay goalposts. One day I caught the manly bass having a girlie hissy fit in the communal kitchen. He was waging war with an uncooperative cheese soufflé while wearing a plaid, lace-ruffled apron. Meanwhile the castrato was upstairs drilling big holes in the wall above their living room window in preparation for the hanging of some fancy poof draperies, which, to add to the confusion, the bass had been sewing and ruching that very morning. It was not long before we were forced to admit that we had no idea who was Boris and who was Doris.

Poofs, homos, queers, friends of Dorothy, call them what you will, this strange club, of which Biddie and I were now members, was turning out to be far more nuanced than we had ever envisaged. We were having a hard time finding a niche, let alone a date. Our mockery of Boris and Doris concealed a tinge of envy. Despite their little anomalies, Boris and Doris had found happiness: they were content with themselves and with each other.

We, by contrast, were immature, inexperienced, and fairly dreadful at conducting relationships. I had recently been dating another window dresser. It did not last long. He invited me over one night and announced that he had decided to 'set me free'. I was so naïve that I actually said, 'Good heavens, how considerate!' and left his apartment feeling fluffy and light-headed and grateful. It took me months to figure out I had been dumped.

Biddie was even more inexperienced than I was. Not long after we moved to London, an attractive man had approached him on the Underground and invited him to 'come back for coffee'. Biddie had immediately blown it.

'I'm afraid I don't drink coffee' was his doltish reply.

I tried to persuade him that 'come back for coffee' was a common euphemism. 'Daughter! It's just a polite way of inviting you back for a bit of slap and tickle, that's all.'

'But, daughter! As you yourself know, I don't *drink* coffee! Don't you get it! I prefer tea,' he kept saying.

Biddie refused to acknowledge that this person had any intention other than to force gallons of ghastly unwanted coffee down his throat.

The problem was that my roommate and I both had very 1950s ideas about dating: we were wildly out of step with the burgeoning 1970s gay culture. Our concept of romance was based on Deborah Kerr and Burt Lancaster embracing on the beach in *From Here to Eternity,* or Liz Taylor and Monty Clift in *A Place in the Sun.* We were conventional. Not so the people we met. Most gay men seemed to have *proclivities.*

One evening while strolling home up Portobello Road, I was approached by a uniformed policeman. Instead of arresting me, he asked me to come home for a glass of sherry. He was handsome and charming, so I accepted. Imagine Biddie's face when I tell him about this, I thought as we sped into the night in his panda car with me in the back looking like a rather unmenacing felon.

We drove to a very chic house in smart W8. I noted with surprise that the decor was quite fancy.

Drinks were proffered, after which the police uniform was discarded, only to be replaced by another uniform, this time from Her Majesty's Coldstream Guards. I began to suspect that the whole police thing, including the panda car, was some elaborate, well-financed fetish. A closet full of uniforms was unfurled, confirming my suspicions. I fled.

On another occasion, Biddie and I decided to check out the late-night cruising scene on Hampstead Heath. We had heard about the naughty goings-on from friends. Nothing could have prepared us for the kinky spectacle we encountered.

We clutched on to each other and giggled our way through the nocturnal autumn mists. Suddenly Biddie dug his fingers into my arm. 'Look up,' he whispered, 'and try not to scream.'

I followed his instructions. Then I saw it. There, glistening in the moonlight, was a chubby man encased head to foot in a black rubber catsuit sitting on a not very sturdy branch.

Biddie waved. The rubber person chose not to wave back. He just sat there like a horrid, shiny tree fungus.

Though we were greatly amused, the whole experience left us feeling rather ordinary. Instead of thinking, What's wrong with all these deranged perverts? we thought, What is wrong with us?

How come we weren't riddled with kinky inclinations? How come we weren't sitting in a tree on Hampstead Heath encased in latex? Were we somehow retarded in our development?

With our mid-century ideas of romance, we felt somewhat alienated.

At least we had each other.

Despite the occasional bout of sisterly bickering, Biddie and I got along well. From the perspective of Jamaican Lady across the street, we must have seemed like such a happy duo, or trio if you count Biddie's alter ego.

I was the busy, dynamic window dresser, the shorter of the three, who trudged home from work each night, frequently carrying strange props – ostrich feathers, Pierrot masks, and Chinese fans, all 'borrowed' from the display studio at my place of employ.

Biddie was, from Jamaican Lady's perspective, probably my femmy partner. He wore tightly cinched paramilitary jumpsuits, pink plastic sandals and a vintage poodle sweater. He came and went at odd hours, a bit like Jamaican Lady herself.

Then, last but not least, there was Biddie's sophisticated twin sister. She stayed at home all day and emerged every evening sporting chiffon and vintage satin gowns with long, trailing flyaway panels. These gossamer wings frequently got caught in the front door when she strode out on her nightly sorties. The short window dresser always seemed to derive an enormous amount of amusement from the subsequent whiplash.

This nocturnal, angular glamour puss was sometimes accompanied by the short window dresser but was never, for some strange reason, seen in the company of her slightly shorter twin. I'm sure this was quite perplexing to Jamaican Lady.

The truth of the matter was that, in less than a year, Biddie had become a successful and much-sought-after drag cabaret performer. While Jamaican Lady was flashing pedestrians, motorists and the occasional bloke in a wheelchair, Biddie was over on the swanky side of town beguiling audiences in trendy clubs and restaurants.

London was, at this particular time, bursting at the

seams with drag queens. They were mostly bawdy types, with names like Dockyard Doris and Bertha Venation, who lip-synched to cassette tapes of Shirley Bassey and brayed obscenities at the audience: 'The owner of this pub is an Irish count – at least I think that's what they called him! Mwaaah!'

Biddie might have been born in a council flat, but he wasn't common like the other London drag queens. His chic, sophisticated stage persona set him apart from the bawdy pub trannies. He never lip-synched: he sang all his songs himself. And he had a gimmick: he changed hats for every song.

'When the Swallows Come Back to Capistrano' was performed with a giant flock of blue glitter swallows circling his head attached by wires. For 'Shakin' the Blues Away' he wore a three-foot-wide Erté-esque number, which was festooned with cascades of blue bugle beads. The actual changing of the hats was accomplished while distracting the audience with a welter of chatty badinage: 'Ladies! I find the best way to get over a man is to get under another one. Don't you?' Biddie's themed chapeaux were designed and constructed by Biddie himself, using glue, spit and stolen display paraphernalia. Word spread. Young trendies flocked from all over London to see Biddie and His Amazing Hats.

In tandem with his growing fan base, Biddie was developing a scary addiction. It was causing me considerable concern. If we had had such things as interventions back then, I would have undoubtedly called Doreen and Cyril Biddlecombe up to London and staged one.

It wasn't Biddie's fault. He was only human. He was young and susceptible and totally caught up in the magical, decadent whirl of *cabaret*.

Like so many addictions, it started innocently enough.

Every time he performed, admirers would ply Biddie with booze. Who doesn't love a free drink, especially when it is accompanied by an avalanche of post-performance praise? Biddie liked any tipple as long as it was brightly coloured. His faves were sugary showgirl drinks like Parfait Amour (purple) and Chartreuse (yellow-green). These evil pushers would wait until he was well lubricated, and then they would pounce. No, I'm not talking about pills or smack or cocaine. It was something far more pernicious.

They would offer him their unwanted upright pianos.

Before TV and hi-fi, every home in England had an upright piano in the parlour. During wartime the beleaguered Brits had steadied their nerves by pounding out uplifting ditties like 'Hang Out Your Washing on the Siegfried Line' and 'Roll Out the Barrel'. In the 1960s these instruments acquired a certain nostalgia chic: trendy people tore the fronts off, painted them white, and stuck daisies and geraniums on them or in them.

Now all these trendy types, none of whom could even play the piano, had started to begrudge the space. But what to do? Nobody had the heart to throw Granny's old piano out onto the street. Here was the perfect solution: unload your upright piano onto your local transvestite cabaret entertainer.

When the first one arrived *chez nous*, Biddie was delirious. No more expensive rehearsal rooms! He immediately set about honing his routines and learning tonnes of new songs. Everything was rosy and peachy. We even found room for the now-displaced floor pillow. We wedged it on top of the piano, where it provided additional sound-proofing.

I was quite taken aback when, unannounced, a second piano arrived on our doorstep. I began to suspect that he might be hooked. He was. When it came to upright pianos, Biddie was a sitting duck. These evil manipulators only had to wait until he was in convivial après-show mode. Once he had a couple of crèmes de menthe (green) inside him, they knew he was too weak to resist.

'Oh, daughter, I've done it again,' he would admit groggily upon waking and realising that yet one more piano was on its way.

At the time of the pudding incident, Biddie had accumulated three pianos. A fourth was due any day.

I was not the only person concerned about this turn of events. Biddie's addiction was giving our landlady, a pixie-sized Italian lady called Mrs Rizzo, chronic indigestion. She had every reason to be concerned. Her building was already crumbling: every time we banged the front door, large chunks of masonry fell from the edifice. The weight of

Biddie's burgeoning piano collection had the potential to demolish the building from the inside. Biddie's pianos became Mrs Rizzo's obsession.

Our long-suffering landlady had a metal pin in her hip, which slowed her down considerably and made her seem to us as if she was part of Monty Python's 'Ministry of Silly Walks'. Despite her handicap, she managed to ambush Biddie quite successfully on a number of occasions. She would wait until he was dressed up like a Christian Dior fashion portrait circa 1951 and corner him as he tore through the hallway.

'My joists! My joists!' she would scream up at the fleeing Biddie, who, in heels, was approximately twice her height. She would then stagger after her cross-dressing tenant Biddie, clutching at his flyaway chiffon panels, and chase him into his waiting taxi.

Occasionally I would accompany Biddie to his gigs. It was fun watching people screaming and applauding. I was proud of my showbiz room-mate. I would do my best to insert myself between him and his pushers. But I couldn't be there every night.

More often than not I would stay at home and hang out with our neighbours. We would while away the evening in conversation, which sounds very quaint and intellectual but was really a function of the fact that there was a recession and nobody had a television, not even Boris and Doris.

Having been born in a rooming house, and grown up surrounded by miscellaneous lodgers and relatives, I

enjoyed hobnobbing and chatting with our fellow tenants
and finding out about their lives. I had my eye on an
American college student from LA who lived on the
second floor. He was attractive in a blond and Aryan
lumberjack sort of way. I was a little confused by his
hypermasculine appearance. Was he one of us? There
were no girlfriends in evidence. Maybe he was just a nice
bloke who was waiting for Miss Right to come along.

One night he tapped on my door and invited me up to
share his dinner.

'Good luck, daughter! Zip me up before you go, would
you?' said Biddie, who was sponging Pan-Cake onto his
giraffe neck.

With an air of cautious anticipation, I prepared for
what I hoped was a date. I threw on the 1920s silk satin
dressing gown I wore when lounging around the house. It
was pale blue and printed with Art Deco fans in black,
yellow and pink. Very Noël Coward, you might say.
Having purchased this exquisite vintage item for a mere
ten pennies at a jumble sale, I was extremely proud of it.

A dressing gown for a date? Why not? What could be
more normal than walking around the house in a towelling
kimono, a damask peignoir, or a nice rayon robe? Dressing
gowns seemed perfectly acceptable to me. Like dentures,
they were a huge part of my childhood. Even though we
lived on a busy bus route, my parents were frequently to be
seen weeding the front yard or greeting the postman in
their dressing gowns.

The evening seemed, at least from my point of view, to be going quite well. Within the first twenty minutes I knocked back most of Mr LA's Chablis. Dates are fun! I really should do this more often, I thought.

Feeling warm, tingly and confident, I flashed a bit of leg and put my hand inside his flannel shirt. I touched his hairy chest with tentative fingers. He removed my hand.

Mr LA smiled, and then, in a lengthy and caring exposition which suggested that he might have had a little too much psychotherapy, he explained to me why he had no interest in dating men who swished round the house in Noël Coward dressing gowns. The psychobabble was worse than a more traditional rebuke. If he had said, 'Keep your slimy paws to yourself!' I could have handled it. All this stuff about 'boundaries' and 'personal choices' was making me feel even more leprous. Rubbing salt into the wound, he added that he never dated short personages.

Feeling a bit like a third-rate travelling theatrical midget, I thanked him profusely and staggered back down to our hovel.

I picked up Happy Harry and in an irate sardonic fashion began to re-enact the painful conversation.

'It's just not my scene, man . . . I'm not judgemental . . . The vibe I'm getting from you . . .'

This was my first close encounter with gay fascism. Still wearing Noël Coward and still clutching Happy Harry, I crawled into bed and prayed for oblivion.

Despite the lack of mutual erotic chemistry, Mr LA and

I continued to hang out. It was an odd symbiosis. I had a record player and no albums. We had been robbed while living next to Rita the tart. The thieves had left the floor pillow but taken all our record albums and an old radio with Braille knobs which Aunt Phyllis had passed on to me.

The Lumberjack had one single record album and no record player. It was the historic LaBelle record entitled *Nightbirds*, which ironically, featured the astoundingly great song with the line 'Voulez-vous coucher avec moi, ce soir?' We bopped along with it, safe in the knowledge that, thanks to my dressing gown and lack of height, we would not coucher ce soir, or any other soir.

As we played the album over and over, Mr LA regaled me with tales of gay life in America, the discos, the saunas, the Warhol crowd. He was obsessed with a new John Waters movie that had recently premiered in Greenwich Village starring an obese transvestite named Divine. The movie was called *Pink Flamingos:* le tout New York was talking about it because, in the last scene, Divine kneels down on the pavement and eats poodle faeces. I guffawed appreciatively but was secretly appalled.

I have always had an ambivalent relationship with dog faeces. If my sister and I wanted to play in the backyard, we first had to clean up Lassie's poo. This activity invariably left me nauseated and appetite-less.

Lassie was my blind aunt Phyllis's golden Lab. A worthier and more lovely canine it would be hard to find. My sister and I were deeply in love with her. We would lie by the fire with Lassie, spooning and cuddling and playing with her silky ears. I held her paws and wrote her Christmas cards and kissed her until I got worms. And then kissed her again. When she died we were inconsolable. Despite the strength of my passion, any contact with her faecal matter would send me retching into the delphiniums.

One hot August night, I found I had the house to myself. Biddie was performing, so were Boris and Doris. Mr LA was out looking for other tall blond Aryans. The house was quiet. I donned Noël Coward and embarked on a bit of half-hearted housework.

I started with our minibar-sized refrigerator, which, thanks to months of neglect, had become quite smelly. I began throwing half-eaten horrors into the garbage. At the back of the middle shelf was a large obstruction. Upon further inspection I discovered an untouched Christmas pudding presented to me by Betty Doonan nine months prior.

'You'll need to steam it for about six hours,' said my mother, as if she seriously thought I might devote an evening to pudding steaming.

There was no point in waiting until Betty discovered it on her next visit and berated us for being a couple of 'ungrateful bleeders'. Donning a pair of bright-yellow rubber gloves, I started to scrape the rich-brown, claylike substance out of the bowl.

I felt glad to have the substantial membrane separating my hands from the pudding mix. I never liked to touch anything slimy. As a child I could not understand those kids who insisted on eating with their fingers. Why would anyone in his right mind want to touch shepherd's pie or chocolate pudding?

The only thing worse than touching food is touching poo, I mused.

An idea was taking shape in my head.

As I clawed and scraped at the thick mass, I could smell my mother's cooking sherry. Mmmm! It reminded me of butch men's aftershave.

I continued to scrape and muse.

This pudding smelled so much better and more enticing than Lassie's poo, and yet how similar of texture.

I had no idea just how similar until I absentmindedly rolled a handful of pudding into a torpedo shape. Good heavens! If there was ever a competition to create the world's most convincing dog poo facsimile, Betty's Xmas pudding would win hands down. It was much more real-looking than the glossy, caramel-coloured fake doggy doo that is sold to delighted customers at joke shops the world over.

Meanwhile, in some smoky boîte on the other side of town, Biddie was taking a well-earned break from performing. He had just belted his way through 'Bali Ha'i' and was desperate to remove the cumbersome revolving desert island he wore to perform this number. He had made the Bali Ha'i hat himself from three rolls of Mrs Rizzo's toilet paper. He mashed the paper up with flour and water, formed it into an island shape, and then baked it in the oven. After about ten minutes it burst into flames, filling the house with horrid smoke and bringing Boris and Doris onto their landing. Unperturbed, Biddie waited for Bali Ha'i to cool. After skillfully covering the charred areas in paint, he glued a Barbie-sized palm tree next to it, secured the entire thing to a revolving cake stand, et voilà! Bali Ha'i! This number was always a huge hit. Tonight had been no exception: Biddie was deluged with fans and piano owners.

Meanwhile, *chez nous*, I was quivering with a mixture of excitement, mirth and revulsion. I thought I might burst. The object of my attention was now sitting in the middle of a large expanse of Mrs Rizzo's white linoleum floor.

I had fashioned two or three handfuls of pudding into an exquisitely accurate reproduction of dog poo. It looked exactly like one of dear old Lassie's deposits. I then placed my little sculpture directly in Biddie's path. He would be bound to see it as soon as he walked in, even if he was plastered. I did not want him to slip in it. He was a bit accident prone and quite likely to fall and crack his skull on the nearest piano.

I stared at my creation with a mixture of horror and excitement. This would surely be the greatest practical joke in the history of our relationship. People might think of Biddie as the vivacious one, the bubbly showbiz entertainer, but when push came to shove, it was I, his shorter, less scintillating room-mate, who had come up with the craziest gag of all time.

Suddenly, one turd rolled mysteriously away from the main cluster. Had the spirit of Lassie entered the room? I was about to restore it to its former position when I realised that this new spontaneous configuration had only added to the overall verisimilitude of my poo facsimile.

I turned out the lights and leapt into bed to await Biddie's return.

He did not come home.

I nodded off.

Two hours later I was awakened by the slamming of a cab door. I could hear Biddie dump his suitcase full of hats on the front doorstep. Eventually he found his keys and, with the urgency that only a homecoming transvestite in a rough neighbourhood can understand, dived through the open front door and slammed it behind him, precipitating another masonry fall.

The evil anticipation of the practical joker returned to me through the fog of sleepiness. With darting eyes and baited breath, I waited for the inevitable bloodcurdling scream.

'EEEEEEEEE!!!!! Oh, my God! Daughter! Wake up! Was there a bloody dog in here?'

I clicked on my light, squinted across the room, and addressed my begowned room-mate. 'Get a grip, daughter. What the hell are you talking about?'

Biddie was pointing a long, cocktail-gloved finger at the offending object, which, spotlit on Mrs Rizzo's white vinyl, was impossible to miss.

'Is it really poo?' I asked with genuine concern, leaping out of bed and belting Noël Coward around me. 'Let's take a closer look.'

Adopting a Sherlock Holmes-ish air, I got down on my knees and sniffed. 'Odourless excrement! How unusual. We may need to get it analysed.'

'It's shit, you idiot! Get away from it,' advised Biddie.

'Let's try and keep our heads, shall we? There's only one sure way to find out,' I said authoritatively. Gingerly, I picked up an hors d'oeuvre-sized portion.

Biddie screamed.

I raised the poo to my lips.

Biddie gasped.

I nibbled with a concerned, connoisseurial air.

Biddie screamed again.

Slowly I began to masticate the pudding/poo, accompanied by more neighbour-rousing screams from Biddie.

I was starting to feel slightly sick.

'Want to try some?' I said wanly.

We then stared at each other for about three seconds, which doesn't sound like a really long time but is, especially when you have a mouthful of faux poo.

I then spat the pudding into an old tissue, which I found in Noël Coward's pocket.

Where were the peals of laughter? Where was the thigh-slapping acknowledgement of my genius?

There was nothing. Only the ticking of Mrs Rizzo's reproduction Victorian hall clock.

My carefully contrived practical joke was so unfunny that all we could do was stare at each other. Biddie was not amused. Or appalled. He was strangely indifferent. As was I. Even Happy Harry was a no comment.

The brilliant stunt I had anticipated would keep us rolling in the aisles for months had not only fallen flat. Somehow it had never existed.

'Christmas pudding! You are naughty. Make us a cuppa,' said Biddie and began scraping off his maquillage. I cleaned up the torpedoes of pudding and flushed them down the toilet.

Almost immediately we moved on. Biddie regaled me with the highlights of his evening. He had met a fabulous couple who'd bought him pink champagne and had, oh so generously, offered him their old upright piano. He told them he would have to think about it. I enthusiastically applauded these attempts to kick his addiction.

Then we had a nice cup of tea, after which I went to bed and dreamt of Lassie.

★
★

Chapter 12

NO KNICKERS

O UR HEARTS sank when we saw it. Number 230 Edna Street was a painfully ordinary two-storey terraced house with a bay window and minuscule front garden. England is full of such houses. They are the epitome of British respectability.

Biddie and I had not come to London to be respectable or ordinary. That was the whole point. We had come to London to have a smashing time and wear outrageously groovy clobber and to lounge on floor pillows with the Beautiful People while eating lotuses and guzzling champers.

Number 230 Edna Street was not what we had in mind.

But we didn't have much choice. Rental flats were in short supply. And, delusions of grandeur aside, we knew we were lucky to get it.

We would just have to make it extraordinary.

The humble, unprovocative exterior could not be changed. We would have to ignore it or, better yet, throw it into sharp contrast. That was it! Instead of capitulating to the crushing ordinariness of the exterior, we would fight it tooth and nail. We would create a dazzlingly dissonant interior. We would create a cesspool of unmitigated decorative excess.

First stop: Biddie's boudoir.

We began by tenting the ceiling with miles of navy and purple polyester satin. We cut the fabric in lengths and gathered them into the centre of the room, forming a giant sphincter. This confluence of fabric was secured around the top of a crappy brass Moroccan light fixture. The rich swathes of synthetic satin were then stapled to the perimeter picture rail. The fullness billowed down, evoking the ceiling of a Bedouin tent. The walls were then draped with synthetic moirés and brocades, window display fabrics 'borrowed' from my various places of employ. Mirrors were interspersed among the fabrics to create the illusion of infinite space. The concept was inspired by Léon Bakst's famous design for the Ballets Russes production of *Scheherazade*. With my staple gun and Biddie's soft-furnishings experience, we did Diaghilev proud.

In the middle of the room, upon mounds of nylon-lamé-covered cushions and tasselled throws, lay Scheherazade herself, a.k.a. Biddie. Here he lolled for hours, listening to Yma Sumac* records, making phone calls in a regal kind of way, and trying to pretend that he could not hear the traffic from Battersea High Street in the distance.

Happy Harry was always within arm's reach. Time had not been kind to Happy Harry. His bow tie was missing, his suit was food-stained, and there was a hairline crack in his skull. With this loss of looks came a loss of power: he no longer had the ability to make me question my sanity.

The floor pillow, which seemed quite pedestrian in this exotic environment, was plonked next to the bed. Biddie now used it as a vide-poche, valet and nightstand.

In the four corners of the room, sitting upon gold-painted Styrofoam columns, were four large, shiny black-amoor statues. They were Vac-U-Form plastic and weighed about two ounces each. These 'antiquities' came from a window display at the Wallis shop on Oxford

---

*Yma Sumac: a glamorous songstress. Back in the 50s, when Yma and her 5-octave range burst onto the scene, her press releases claimed that she was a Peruvian princess. She said she had grown up in the Andes, surrounded by eagles and panthers. Rumours subsequently abounded that this was pure fantasy and that she was just a nice girl from Brooklyn called Amy Camus, who had reversed her name.

Street. Armfuls of peacock feathers, from a window display at Aquascutum on Regent Street, shot out of the tops of their heads like exploding volcanoes.

Biddie initiated much of this insanity. My contribution was the props. I was a busy window dresser with access to all kinds of tchotchkes and gewgaws, which we enthusiastically funnelled into our abode.

The prop-filled bathroom was inspired by our time at Butlins. A whole Tippi Hedren of fake birds of various sizes – lifelike rubber parakeets and evil-looking egrets – dangled from the ceiling on monofilament. All other surfaces were covered in bright green AstroTurf. The bath was surrounded by ramparts of plastic flowers.

These rooms prompted us to stage endless photo sessions, the results of which I have preserved for posterity. I pore over them once in a while and marvel at our highbrow-lowbrow theatrical chutzpah. Here's me, dancing through Biddie's room dressed up as Nijinsky. There's Biddie as Ophelia, drowning in the bathtub in a filmy negligee and a long auburn wig. Here's me and Biddie in a Versailles tableau: he's in a pale-blue chintz eighteenth-century court gown, which we made from a bolt of fabric we found under the stairs, and I'm dressed as his blackamoor, looking not unlike the window display props in Biddie's bedroom.

Within a relatively short period of time we had succeeded in creating our own alternative universe. As with the Malaysian Simulator, it was a place where we always felt happy and squishy and safe. We kept reality at bay by never reading newspapers and never acquiring a TV.

This living diorama of hokey costumes and staple-gunned sets was the ultimate defence against the horrors of the world and, more importantly, the gritty ordinariness of our working-class neighbourhood. On the adjacent high street, in the cold light of day, grim-faced housewives with dangling cigarettes scowled at us disapprovingly and shop-keepers frequently addressed Biddie, with a 'Good morning, madam – oops, I mean, sir!' In the evening, when we got dolled up for a night on the town, gangs of horrid youths would chase us down the street, forcing us to escape onto double-decker buses which were heading in the opposite direction to that we intended. Thank God we had our Red Rover bus passes! But more on those later.

We were not the only nellies in the neighbourhood. Far from it. There was, coincidentally, another window dresser living upstairs, a soigné gentleman *d'un certain age*. He, to his everlasting regret, was the acquaintance who had alerted us about this apartment when it had fallen vacant.

This upstairs window dresser, a former civil servant, trimmed the window displays at various genteel Bond Street emporiums. He was good-looking and charming, and, despite his age, enjoyed the attentions of a handsome live-in lover, who was considerably his junior.

The upstairs window dresser augmented his window-dressing income with money earned from regular photographic modelling assignments. With his elegant manners and waxed moustache, he represented an archetype that has all but disappeared but was, back then, a staple of advertising imagery: I refer to the *sophisticated older gentleman*.

He was the man with the greying temples – a colonel, a bishop, or a butler pouring Tio Pepe into guests' glasses. There he was again, enjoying a cigarillo, or helping a silver-haired, bitchy-looking lady into a white mink stole as they both contemplated their gleaming new Bentley. The upstairs window dresser played his roles with aplomb. He had a posh, snooty air, which was perfect for marketing the *finer things of life*.

The upstairs window dresser kept all his old display props in a shed in our backyard. We loved to watch him rummaging through his extensive repertoire in search of inspiration. There was nothing radical or avant-garde about his displays. They were both wildly appropriate and relentlessly seasonal: autumn leaves, spring blossoms, Easter lilies, etc. We could track the seasons by watching his activities. We did not really believe that summer was over until we saw him dragging out that sack of plastic acorns and that stuffed squirrel.

Though his displays were rather predictable, the upstairs window dresser's apartment was exquisite and unbelievably chic. He had Jacobean side tables and Fornasetti plates. There were no plastic blackamoors plonked around his bed. He would never have dreamt of incorporating display props into his residential decor.

We were the opposite. *All* of my window displays – every single prop and ostrich feather – went straight into our house, elevating each room to new heights of excess and cheesiness.

Nowhere was the window dresser's 'Art' more shamefully evident than in my own room. While Biddie's room recalled the glories of Byzantium, mine evoked the decadent opium dens of 19th century China.

I covered the walls in raging red Chinois wallpaper and slapped red gloss paint on everything I could get my paws on. To finish it off, I hung an oversized red and gold paper Chinese lantern from the ceiling.

The light was on most of the time because I never opened the curtains.

The other houses in Edna Street had net curtains which were swagged back, proudly displaying decorating styles which, with the exception of the upstairs window dresser's, recalled the frowzy mod interior of Doreen Biddlecombe's parlour.

Though my room faced directly onto the pavement of Edna Street, I was determined to deny the fact. I draped and swagged that front window to within an inch of its life, blotting out the painful reality that lurked on the other side.

Rather than bother with all the usual rails and hooks and curtain rods, I took a shortcut. I *glued* the curtains in place. Taking my trusty glue gun, I dribbled hot glue along the wall and the top of the window frame. And then I glued them in place. Burgundy crushed velvet they were, discarded from a tailor's-shop window display on Savile Row.

'By the year 2000 everyone will be hanging their drapes like this,' I cackled as I hacked and adhered my magnificent curtains into place in under 20 minutes. To hide the enormity of my crime, I hot-glued some additional whooshes of fabric along the top. This not only hid the blobs of glue and the raw edges but added an instant – albeit somewhat un-Chinese – baroque flourish.

One day our landlord, a nice man who lived in fancy Chelsea digs across the river, stopped by to collect the rent. He took one look at my glue-gunned curtains and let out a high-pitched, piglike sound. He turned pale and then puce. 'All fur coat and no knickers. That's what you two are!'

I was taken aback. We were very proud of our relentlessly overdecorated pad, and quite certain that nowhere else in London offered a greater contrast between the outside and the inside.

He stared at my glue-gunned drapes and looked at me as if I were the Antichrist.

'All fur coat and no knickers!'

For the younger reader: this stinging indictment was used at the time to describe a person whose flashy façade hid a multitude of stylistic and moral deficiencies.

The grieving, confused landlord then turned his attention to the toilet, now Afro-themed and covered in snakeskin wallpaper. The flush was operated with the aid of a dangling Tarzan vine. Inventive though our decor might have been, it could not distract the landlord from the rust-stained toilet bowl. He yanked back the raffia blind which covered the tiny window of our toilet. A shaft of unforgiving light penetrated our fantasy world.

'Look at the filth!' he gasped.

After one more 'all fur coat and no knickers!' he left, crunching off down the gravel path.

He was right. It was filthy. We had neither the money for a cleaning lady nor the inclination to do the job ourselves. Our incentive to clean was zero. None of our guests ever commented on the dirt. Our excessive decor rendered the subject irrelevant.

Biddie and I justified our aversion to housework by quoting Quentin Crisp, the famously blue-rinsed bohemian who lived across the river in Fulham. Mr Crisp in his autobiography *The Naked Civil Servant* advised against becoming a slave to cleanliness: 'After four years the dust doesn't get any worse.'

Number 230 Edna Street was a monument to this terrible truism.

Even if we'd had the inclination to clean, we had no time. We were much too busy being fabulous. Biddie and his new singing partner, a voluptuous redhead called Eve Ferrett, had become a fixture on the London scene, specialising in campy standards and retro costumes. They had even appeared on TV.

Eve was busty and glam and had garnered the attention of the press with the aid of two stuffed ferrets – a not very oblique reference to her name – which accompanied her everywhere. The ferrets had wheels attached to their feet and long sticks attached to their bejewelled collars. The sticks gave the illusion of straining leashes and enabled Eve to trundle them in front of her wherever she went. Eve's concept was a low-rent version of those Art Deco statuettes which depict a lady in a cloche hat being pulled along by two elegant greyhounds.

Biddie and Eve and the ferrets got invited to everything that was going on in London. I tagged along. Mad drunken escapades dominated this period of my life. Many's the morning we would roll home with the sun coming up, singing and screeching at the top of our lungs. On one particularly memorable occasion Biddie misplaced his keys. While he fumbled, Eve continued belting out her version of Connie Francis's 50s hit 'Lipstick on Your Collar'. Suddenly the upstairs window flew open.

Whooooooosh!

A deluge of lukewarm liquid brought Eve's singing to a screeching halt.

'Blimey! I can't believe he threw water all over us. Me ferrets are drenched!' said Eve, whose red bouffant was now caving in.

'My dear, let me assure you,' said the always gracious upstairs window dresser, 'this is *not* water.'

The upstairs window dresser was smiling down. In his right hand he held an exquisite Victorian chamber pot.

Nothing was ever quite what it seemed at number 230 Edna Street.

One muggy summer evening there was a knock at the door. Biddie and I exchanged startled glances. Who, or what, would have the audacity to arrive unannounced at our sequined sanctum?

We never had impromptu visitors. Even the upstairs window dresser and his handsome boyfriend would phone before dropping in.

I was in the middle of a sewing job. In my relentless quest for cash, I had rashly taken on the project of sewing the seat cushions, about two hundred in all, for a large West End hair salon. I was in the middle of inserting my 90th zipper.

Biddie, turbaned and moist, had just climbed into the tub in the AstroTurf bathroom. His face was covered in make-up. He had read somewhere that Bianca Jagger applied her make-up before soaking in the tub in order to allow her foundation to 'sink in'. He had become a devotee of this practice.

Anxiously I got up from the sewing machine and went towards the door. Through the mottled glass I discerned a short, amorphous, grey-clad figure. What manner of man or beast was attempting to penetrate our overdecorated inertia? I opened the door. I gasped. I pretended my gasp was a cough.

Here on my doorstep was one of the strangest apparitions I have ever seen.

It spoke.

'Hello. I'm-Grey-flannel-shorts-and-kneesocks-of-North-London-and-I've-come-in-response-to-your-ad,' said the person in a flat, half-hearted kind of way.

I was too stunned to take in the content of what had been said. I was completely and hopelessly sidetracked by this person's appearance.

If clothing is a form of nonverbal communication, before me stood a whole new language.

Grey-flannel-shorts-and-kneesocks-of-North-London was male. He was no longer in the first flush of youth. The contemporary celebrity lookalike who most readily springs to mind would have to be Harold Wilson. Grey-flannel-shorts-and-kneesocks-of-North-London was a pedestrian, portly, grey-haired, middle-aged man, and true to his name, Grey-flannel-shorts-and-kneesocks-of-North-London was wearing grey flannel shorts and kneesocks. A boys' prep school uniform.

I had seen grown people wearing school uniforms before. Many punk rockers on the Kings Road favoured torn, stained school ties and blazers. But this was something new.

First, there was a frightening authenticity and attention to detail. The kneesocks had small tabbed garters, which protruded from under the sock folds. The tie was knotted with the angry, sartorially oblivious nonchalance typical of English schoolboys.

Then there were the shorts: a little too long, but short enough to reveal authentically scraped and scabbed knees. Grey-flannel-shorts-and-kneesocks-of-North-London was giving *schoolboy realness*.

Then I noticed it, the most exquisitely evocative detail of all. Under his left arm, Grey-flannel-shorts-and-kneesocks-of-North-London carried a small bundle of exercise books, from which protruded a twelve-inch ruler. He had homework!

Running his ink-stained, pudgy fingers through his grey mop of hair, the mysterious visitor repeated himself. 'Hello. I'm Grey-flannel-shorts-and-kneesocks-of-North-London-and-I've-come-in-response-to-your-ad.' He sounded like an exhausted novelty-telegram delivery person.

As he spoke I realised that Grey-flannel-shorts-and-kneesocks-of-North-London was suffering from a mild speech impediment. What he had actually said was 'Hello. I'm gwey flannel shorts and kneesocks of Nowth London and I've come in wesponse to youw ad.'

He breathed a sigh of petulant, boyish frustration.

'I'm twying to find someone called James. Are you James?'

My blood ran cold.

Oh! My God! Biddie's name was James!

Suddenly I saw it all. Jimmy Biddlecombe, my child-hood friend (fwend), had, unbeknownst to me, developed a really disturbing proclivity.

I was shocked.

I scoured my brain for any telltale signs.

Maybe it was Paddy! When we were young school-boys, and wearing grey flannel shorts of our own, there was one particular bus conductor, an Irishman, who used to make a point of pinching and fondling our knees. Known as Paddy, this cheeky funster was absolutely inca-pable of keeping his horrid little hands off our porky legs. Paddy's unwanted attentions had obviously turned Biddie into a big screaming pervert!

I had always thought there was such a strong bond between us. We always told each other everything. And now this!

'Daughter, it's for you, I think,' I said, as I tried not to think about the possibility that Grey-flannel-shorts-and-kneesocks-of-North-London might one day move into our flat and become Mr Biddie.

My turbaned room-mate, complaining bitterly, emerged from the tub and stuck his head round the door. The foundation had sunk in nicely.

'I'm Gwey-flannel-shorts-and-kneesocks. Are you James?'

'Good evening!' ejaculated Biddie, who had become

quite good at handling rowdies and assorted lunatics but now seemed lost for a snappy comeback. 'Oh, luv! I think you might have the wrong house,' suggested Biddie, much to my relief.

Grey-flannel-shorts let out another depressed sigh. He looked quite forlorn, like a child with a broken toy.

'Oh. I've had such a tewible wunawound,' he said, nibbling on his ruler and leaning on the door frame. He relaxed with the air of one who sensed he was among like-minded folk. Our new friend then told us of his long and embarrassing trek from North London, and of various encounters gone awry.

'I've been all over Bwixton and out as far as Wichmond.'

The poignancy of his story enrobed us with feelings of fascinated discomfort. We wanted to know everything, and yet nothing.

'A man in a Cortina took one look at me and dwove off!'

'Oh, men! Well, if it's any comfort to you, we've all been there, daughter!' chimed Biddie in a tone of comforting complicity.

Relaxing more and sweating profusely, Grey-flannel-shorts began to paint a picture of his life. He lived with his mother. She was always mad at him because he never went out to work and always wore a school uniform. In desperation to find love, he had corresponded with some-one in South London via a PO box. All he knew about this person was that he shared Kneesocks's proclivities and that he lived somewhere in Brixton. Kneesocks had been directed to us – somewhat vindictively – after randomly banging on a neighbour's door.

Biddie and I felt a simultaneous surge of empathy. We knew what it was like to feel spurned and reviled. Either one of us could so easily have ended up like Grey-flannel-shorts-and-kneesocks-of-North-London. There but for the grace of God went Biddie and Simon.

'If I'd known it was going to be like this,' he contin-ued, looking down at his own strange little costume as if it were something that someone had forced him to wear, 'I would have bought myself one of those new Wed Wover bus passes.'

Biddie and I smiled and nodded enthusiastically. How could anyone survive without one?

As I contemplated our strange moist visitor on that warm August night, I was overwhelmed by the unfairness and precariousness of life. One false move and you could find yourself wandering round South London in scratchy school uniform with no Red Rover bus pass.

As much as we were fascinated and touched by our new friend, we had no desire to prolong his presence on our front doorstep. One never knew when the upstairs window dresser might get the urge to empty his chamber pot again.

I reached in my pocket and handed Grey-flannel-shorts my nearly expired Red Rover and directed him towards the Number 19 to Finsbury Park. He shoved it into his pocket without saying thanks, which was endearingly schoolboyish.

'I've got a gift for you too,' said Biddie, retreating to his kasbah and re-emerging with Happy Harry.

'Take good care of him. Not too many sweeties. Now run home and do all your homework like a good boy!' said Biddie, who had by now thoroughly entered into the spirit of things, as had I.

'Hurry along!' I said, waving goodbye to the poignant misfit from North London. 'And don't talk to any strangers!'

Chapter 13

PUNKS

T HE SECOND time I was arrested, I was living in Los Angeles and wearing a skirt.

The garment in question was a detachable mini-kilt and was designed to be worn, by both girls and boys, over matching red plaid pants. These were adorned with buckles and zips. Dubbed 'plaid bondage trousers', they were the brainchild of the rebel fashion visionaries Malcolm McLaren and Vivienne Westwood. It was all very 1977 and very punk.

The most striking aspect of this get-up was not the detachable kilt. It was the bondage strap, comprising a loose adjustable belt, which connected the legs at knee level.

This leg strap was less constricting than it appeared. Normal activities – walking, climbing stairs, ice skating (non-competitive), running for the bus, disco dancing, and even driving, which is what I was doing when I was arrested – could be performed while wearing these bondage pants.

I was 27 years old, newly emigrated to America, high on Life and also on something called tequila. Ensconced at the wheel of my hearse-sized, white '65 Dodge station wagon, I felt like a million dollars.

This useful, trusty vehicle played a key role in my window-dressing career. It was invariably crammed with tools, paint pots and a wide assortment of props. At the time of my arrest, I was transporting, among other things, a small taxidermied spider monkey, strings of plastic frankfurters, an oversized fake Oscar made of chicken wire and papier mâché, a bag of fluorescent-hued go-go dancer wigs, and a huge stack of unused vintage colostomy bags. These had been given to me by a nurse friend who had purloined them for me from her place of employ, thinking they might form the basis of an amusing window display. Unable to find a suitable context for such medical oddities, I had driven them around for weeks.

My colostomy bags and I were heading south on Alvarado Street, through the much-sung-about MacArthur Park. It was after midnight, and I was weaving. My nonconformist manoeuvrings were not the result of a tangled bondage strap. I would have loved to have blamed my poor driving on my outfit: 'Your Honour, it was my punk couture . . .' But it wasn't the strap. It was the hooch.

Two motorcycle cops with flashing lights appeared in my rearview mirror. I pulled over and pressed the button that read *Park*. My Dodge was the futuristic push-button model.

The two strapping policemen dismounted and swaggered towards me. Handsome, chiselled and bursting out of their skintight uniforms, these two intimidating specimens were straight out of a Tom of Finland homoerotic drawing.

One officer eyed the stuffed monkey lounging on the red vinyl seat next to me. The other politely asked me to step out of my 'vehicle'. Whenever the word *vehicle* is used, it is safe to assume that things are about to become a great deal less fabulous.

There was no time to detach my kilt or undo my strap. Affecting an upbeat, cooperative, breezy demeanour, I simply swung my legs out of the car as daintily as possible and hoped for the best.

Both cops were about one foot taller than me. They looked me up and down. And up and down. And down and up.

It was spring.

The Santa Ana wind ruffled my mini-kilt.

They stopped looking at me and exchanged bemused

glances. There was a pause. And then it started. They began to giggle. Here were two of the butchest-looking cops in America – straight out of *CHiPs* – and they were tittering like a couple of birdbrained schoolgirls.

Something was going horribly wrong. It wasn't supposed to be like this. In fact, this was the very opposite of what Vivienne and Malcolm had planned when they conceived of my punky plaid bondage trousers. They were not designed to be funny. I was supposed to look alienated, aggrieved, postnuclear and maybe even just a titchy bit intimidating.

Nobody was supposed to giggle.

Eventually my two new pals got their mirth under control.

'So what's with the kilt?' said Cop Number 1 somewhat rhetorically, while chewing tobacco. I was unable to furnish him with a response. Instead I embarked on an enthusiastic, somewhat slurred, autobiographical ramble. I explained that I had recently moved from London to Los Angeles – 'What a great city! Lucky me!' – and that back in the United Kingdom everyone, simply everyone, was wearing plaid bondage trousers. The giggling resumed.

Cop Number 2 finally got a grip.

'Time to walk the line, buddy,' he said, crossing his massive forearms. I lurched into the middle of the pavement and separated my legs. My strap dangled into view.

The giggling resumed once more. The giggling turned to seizures, and the seizures became convulsions.

I began to walk forwards, placing one Doc Marten boot in front of the other as best I could. The kilt swung and the strap dangled and then straightened.

My memory of exactly what happened next is, thanks to the tequila, a bit foggy. I do, however, recall quite distinctly that one of the cops was slapping the seat of his cycle with uncontrollable laughter, while his colleague did the same thing on the hood of my Dodge. Or was he actually lying on the ground, slapping the pavement? I don't quite recall. Either way, my new friends had completely abandoned all attempts to appear authoritarian.

Suddenly the action begins to fast-forward.

The paddy wagon arrives, and the giggly rapport comes screeching to a halt. Handcuffs are applied, contributing substantially to the bondage theme of my attire.

I bid farewell to CHiPs.

'Thanks for everything!' I say in a sincere and desperate attempt to put an optimistic spin on a really dire situation.

On the surface I appear cheery. Internally, I am in a state of screaming desperation. As far as I can tell, my life is completely and utterly over. I am heading for the Big House, and I am wearing a skirt. Within 24 hours I will be massaging the feet of some incarcerated Hells Angel, having become his *Bitch!* For life! *Forever!*

'Get a grip, daughter!' I say to myself as the paddy wagon lurches off into the night.

All is not lost. I am an adaptable kind of person. I will adjust to life in prison. Anything is better than being ignominiously deported back to England. I had left all my London pals on such a glamorous up note. Being forcibly repatriated, with my bondage strap between my legs, only months after having left is more than I can bear. I decide that I would prefer to rot in an American jail in the tattooed arms of some uncouth brute.

I brace myself for the first round of humiliations down at the station. 'If only they had not handcuffed me,' I say to myself as I sit in the back of the wagon looking like a wretched Weegee photograph, 'I could have detached my kilt and bondage strap and stuffed them inside my jacket.' Without the use of my hands, I am unable even to arrange my kilt into a more discreet configuration. It is fanning out from knee to knee like a big old . . . skirt.

Hopefully, when we get to the station, I will be unhandcuffed and permitted to adjust my outfit, thereby rendering it less incendiary and provocative.

But we aren't going to the station.

For two or three hours we drive around picking up more drunks, many of whom are a great deal less savoury than myself.

They are a diverse bunch. Some are down and out, some are upscale, some are vomiting, and some are members of Mexican *cholo* gangs. The latter, with their hairnets, baggy trousers and teardrop tattoos have a panache and originality that rivals my own.

All of my fellow drunks have one thing in common. They are all fascinated by my plaid bondage ensemble.

I affect what I imagine to be a doltish masculine demeanour and pretend to be a mute.

Finally, the paddy wagon fills up. We then drive to the jail in downtown LA, where we are all breathalyzed and thrown in the slammer.

After five minutes behind bars, all I can think about are the repeat offenders. Why? Why? Why? Being incarcerated is such a vile experience that it is impossible to understand the whole concept of career criminals. It goes against every notion of human psychology. There is *nothing* delicious or hip about being locked up. It is smelly, incredibly scary and horribly unfabulous.

After one hour in the holding tank, I have sworn off drink forever and devised all kinds of penances for myself. I will hike ten miles into the desert every Sunday and flagellate myself in a biblical fashion while lying on a sunbaked rock. I will shop at Brooks Brothers for preppy khakis and never wear plaid bondage again. I will walk to Death Valley with dried peas in my shoes. I will go and live with Narg and bake shepherd's pie for her and set her hair with rollers and teach her how to blend her foundation.

Two things save me from becoming the tank bitch.

1. I somehow manage to unclip my skirt and stuff it into my pocket before being thrown in the slammer with all the psychopaths and drug-crazed lunatics.

2. A shrill, cheap-looking hustler who had been arrested for God knows what on Santa Monica Boulevard is monopolising all the available homophobic aggression. He screeches for his lawyer and his mother and starts to drop minor celebrity names. I am probably the only one in the holding tank who has even heard of Melissa Manchester, so it does him very little good.

Inmates snore. Time drags. Inmates belch. Rumours fly. Apparently we are all to be kept inside for at least three days. It is Easter weekend, and there are no officers available to process our paperwork. I lie on a yellowed plastic rubber mattress and think about how soon it will be before I develop hepatitis and my eyeballs turn the same colour as my bed. I dream of freedom. It's been three hours and already I feel like Solzhenitsyn. A large tear rolls down my cheek.

I awake 20 minutes later to the sound of keys clanking and freedom. I am officially charged with *driving under the influence* and given a court date.*

As I walk out into the sunlight, a feeling of unbelievable relief floods my hideously hungover consciousness. I am, give or take a legal problem or two, a free man. I skip

---

*For my court appearance, I wore a nice little suit, a crisp white shirt and a narrow red tie. Next to my giant lawyer I must have looked like an innocent prep school boy, or Happy Harry. Either way, the judge took pity and reduced the charge to reckless driving. I paid, with great difficulty, a nominal fine.

home to the converted garage where I am living in down-town LA.

Once inside I tear off my leather jacket and look in the mirror, expecting to see a long white beard and an ema-ciated visage.

Oh, my God!

I had forgotten about my shirt. This shirt was, in its own way, even more insane than the plaid bondage pants.

It was a forest-green, short-sleeved garment, also from the fertile brain of Ms Westwood. It had a contrasting Peter Pan collar. Emblazoned on the pocket were the words FRIEND OF SID VICIOUS.

Nothing could have been further from the truth. 'Friend of Sid Vicious'! I was not a friend of Sid's nor did I have any intention of being. I had encountered Sid in Vivienne's boutique. I had trembled and left. He was a real punk. I was a mere poseur.

Prior to moving to Los Angeles, I was living with Biddie in Battersea, just over the bridge from Chelsea, the epicen-tre of the punk phenomenon. What 1967 was to the Sum-mer of Love and Haight-Ashbury, 1977 was to the Kings Road and punk.

Punk was a graphic, stylistic revolution which perme-ated everything within screeching distance of South London. There was no way to avoid it. One minute you were a regular person, the next you were wearing a garbage bag, painting your eyes like a raccoon and shoving a safety pin through your ear.

For Biddie and me, every outgoing or homebound journey involved a bus ride down the Kings Road through the punk mayhem which was 1977. Everywhere you looked there were girls wearing leather dresses and black lipstick, and boys wearing T-shirts with nihilistic slogans, torn black jeans, and brothel creepers, the thick-soled shoes that punks appropriated from teddy boys, much to the latter's annoyance.

Everything that had preceded punk, the retro-glamour styles of the early 70s, now seemed pathetic and prissy and completely out of date. Biddie and I had no other choice but to jump on-board. It was *plus grand que nous*.

Biddie's hair was dyed pink and black, which matched most of his clothing. I had my bondage trousers and various other garments. Our friends wore home-made clothes fabricated from Union Jack souvenir shopping bags. We were drowning in punk. And yet there was nothing punk about us. It was just a façade.

As soon as 'God Save the Queen' by the Sex Pistols hit the record stores, we ran out and snagged a copy. Here was the anthem of our times, sung by the anti-hero of the moment. On the record sleeve was the now infamous collage of Her Majesty Queen Elizabeth II with a safety pin stuck through her cheek. Excitedly we took Yma Sumac off the turntable and replaced her with Johnny Rotten and Co.

By the time we got to the bit where Johnny Rotten is screaming *'No future! No future!'* we were rolling our eyes and laughing. It all seemed so insanely camp and funny. An angry adolescent pose. After a while the jackhammering music grated on our nerves. I couldn't wait to pull that disc off the turntable and return to Yma.

We had no idea why the Sex Pistols were advocating anarchy in the first place. We barely knew what anarchy was. Apolitical, TV-less and contentedly superficial, we were oblivious to whatever injustices were fuelling Johnny Rotten's rage.

I tore off my Sid Vicious shirt and my plaid bondage pants as quickly as I could without popping any buttons or breaking any zips, and showered for hours. It didn't help. I still felt utterly putrid. I was a fake. A poseur. A drunk. A felon. I wasn't in a rock band. I was a fey window dresser. And now I was far from home in a town without pity.

I felt a teary pang of homesickness.

Why had I left Biddie and all my friends and family and come to this godforsaken hellhole, where the sun always shines and where nobody in their right mind wears a hot, thick, itchy, plaid skirt?

I shoved my outfit into a plastic garbage bag, never to wear it again.

Autumn 1985 is, for me, a period of great contrasts. At night I crash on the floor of a benevolent friend's place in the East Village. During the day I am working in the legendary Costume Institute at the Metropolitan Museum as display designer for an exhibition called Costumes of Royal India. This is the most fancy-pants job I have ever had.

One day, while fluffing and draping a bejewelled sari, I overhear a colleague mention that the institute has begun to collect clothing designed by Vivienne Westwood. I still have tons of my old outfits, including stuff from the wacky pirate collections of the early 1980s and my arrest ensemble. I cannot imagine wearing any of this stuff again. I dry clean everything and haul it to the Met archive, where it is greeted with shrieks of amused delight.

The soaring values attached to vintage Westwood clothing astound me. Even more shocking is the massive tax refund I receive the following year as a result of my donation. When the shekels arrive, I use them as a down payment on an apartment. So much for Johnny Rotten's anarchy and the destruction of the bourgeoisie!

Fast-forward to 2004. The plaid bondage saga continues, paralleling my own odyssey from confused, marginal pixie to successful, establishment gnome.

The Met Costume Institute stages an exhibition entitled Bravehearts: Men in Skirts. There's a fancy opening party hosted by Jean Paul Gaultier. Much air is kissed and much champagne is guzzled.

I have perfected my own particular brand of *extreme*

air kiss. It involves angling each cheek in the general direction of the kissee, preferably at a distance of at least three feet. My goal is germ avoidance rather than Euro-sophistication. Regarding champagne guzzling, I am even less enthusiastic. I am now teetotal.

I gave up drinking in the mid-80s. It was all quite easy. No Betty Ford. No Alcoholics Anonymous. No 'one day at a time'. I climbed effortlessly onto the wagon after a caring friend informed me, in no uncertain terms, that I was 'slurring like a tragic, drunken old hag'. That did the trick. A sucker for negative reinforcement, I renounced alcohol on the spot.

Clutching a mineral water, I scamper quickly through the exhibition. I am stone-cold sober and acutely aware of it. Attending these kinds of events without the anaes-thetising benefits of alcohol is a nerve-jangling experi-ence. The attendees seem like screeching *Ab Fab* parodies of themselves, i.e. me before I quit the hooch.

Something hauntingly familiar stops me in my tracks.

There, spotlit and resplendent on a teen male mannequin, is my plaid bondage arrest outfit, complete with kilt and strap. I feel as if I have bumped into a rather degenerate, long-lost friend. I let forth a shriek of recognition, garnering the attention of everyone within a ten-yard radius.

I feel a sense of accomplishment and pride. As I regale the adjacent spectators with the whole plaid backstory, I realise that we, I and my skirt, have a great deal in common: we are both survivors. Somehow, more by luck than by judgement, we both managed to stick around long enough to see me reach my half century. Maybe we were just a couple of silly poseurs. So what? The important thing is that we made it. The moths didn't get either of us. It's nothing short of a miracle. We could both so easily have been cut up and used to clean furniture.

Chapter 14

MY WILLIE

I HAD MY FIRST encounter with Death one summer evening in the 1950s.

On this particular occasion my grandmother Narg was having one of her lucid interludes. When these occurred she would ramble through the minutiae of her pre-lobotomy days, recalling strings of mundane facts about her life as a cook and about her two husbands.

I was interested in hearing more about Terry's father. He was a professional astrologer, specialising in mail order horoscopes. Nostradamus Doonan was by all accounts a highly strung young man, who unbeknownst to me at the time, had died by his own hand.

'Where is Grandpa now?' I asked, thinking that Narg should really go and live with him tout de suite. Shouldn't she be cooking his meals and looking after him? She only really needed to visit us once every five years at most.

'He is . . . no longer with us,' replied the unpredictable and mighty Narg, padding on flat feet towards her bedroom.

'He's dead.'

She paused for dramatic effect in her doorway, looking a bit like a badly preserved version of Mrs Danvers in the movie *Rebecca*.

'We'll all be dead one day,' she intoned. 'Even you.'

With that, she vanished into the stygian gloom of her bedroom.

Dead! Up to this point I had been labouring under the happy illusion that Death was something that happened to other people. Good old Narg. She had a real knack for yanking back the curtain on life's fluffy illusions and relieving all within earshot of their most comforting misconceptions.

I was petrified. I had no desire to be, as she put it, *no longer with us*. Apart from anything, it sounded so unnecessarily exclusionary, like being omitted from an invitation list or shut out of a favourite schoolyard game by vindictive playmates.

I went up to bed feeling chilly in my extremities. My room was hot and stuffy and, in contrast to Narg's murky lair on the other side of the house, it was flooded with sunlight. But I still felt cold.

The absolute worst thing about childhood, worse than measles and chicken pox and being sent to an orphanage and psychotic relatives, must surely be having to go to bed with the sun blazing onto one's drapes. Outside the traffic roars, people are laughing and chatting in the street, dogs are barking. Upstairs a five-year-old child lies on his horrid little bed, thinking about Death.

On this particular night I felt as if I were being buried alive.

I tried to imagine what would happen to me when I was *no longer with us*. Was heaven real? Or was it, as with Santa, merely another pathetic illusion about to be exposed by Narg? I ransacked my imagination for visions of heavenly cupids and lyre-twanging angels. Nothing. Only a black abyss.

There was no question that Death must be horrible. I could tell from the way people acted when the subject came up. Nobody wanted to be *no longer with us*. When people sensed that the time had come for them to be *no longer with us*, they never would say, 'Oh, great! My turn. Hand me the lip gloss, would you, luv? Ready! Sayonara, everyone!'

Suddenly I understood the full horror of Death. Nobody wants to go. Everybody goes to his or her Death kicking and screaming.

I clutched my teddy bear and thought about how and when I would meet my end. Overhead I could hear Aunt Phyllis bumping into furniture in her attic room and talking to Lassie, her ageing guide dog. 'Who is the most beautiful girl in the whole wide world? Who is it?'

Animals were not exempt. Phyllis had a box containing snaps of her deceased companions, the loyal furry friends who were *no longer with us*. She treasured these images as if she could see them and wept whenever she spoke their names.

I crawled into bed and stared at the large poster that Uncle Ken had recently brought back from Spain. Ken was going through 'a good period'. He had managed to hold down his job at the local swimming pool long enough to earn a bit of paid holiday. He promptly availed himself of a well-priced package tour to Spain. One week later he returned, sunburnt, slightly dehydrated, and festooned with improbably well-chosen souvenirs: a bag of mangled grapes for the winemakers Betty and Terry, a swashbuckling goat's-hide water canteen with a shoulder strap for my tomboy sister, and a splashy bullfighting poster of the gorgeous El Cordobés for me.

Every night I went to sleep staring at this poster. There was El Cordobés, the handsome post-war bullfighting legend, his manly physique straining inside a pair of fetching skintight yellow britches and matching spangled jacket. Normally this image elicited a warm, tingly feeling in my confused young loins. Not tonight. Tonight El Cordobés, my boyfriend, is about to be gored to death. He would die and I would die and then we would be *no longer with us*.

I began to thrash my head from side to side with my eyes open. El Cordobés see-sawed up and down like a violently rocking fairground ride.

At first I became nauseous. Gradually this rocking motion proved oddly soothing. Eventually, still rocking, I somehow drifted off to sleep. Ditto the following evening. In fact, this is how I went to sleep for years. Every night I thrashed myself to sleep and tried desperately not to think about what it would be like when I was *no longer with us*.

Death was a constant threat. One could be snatched at any time.

One of my sister's classmates was dying of leukaemia. She was ten years old. We visited her and tried to cheer her up. She died soon after.

After her death, my focus shifted. I stopped speculating about what it would be like to be *no longer with us*. I came to terms with the great unknowability of Death. My obsessive thoughts now centred on what might cause me to be *no longer with us*. What dreadful disease or freak accident would be my undoing? If I could figure this out, then maybe I could take preventative action.

Somehow, I managed to elude Death for another year or so. And then it happened. I contracted syphilis. I was ten.

It started one day during a highly unriveting history lesson. We were plodding through Tudor England.

'Henry the Eighth had a massive, weeping sore on his leg caused by syphilis!' yelled our bombastic headmaster.

One by one, he scrutinised our faces for some kind of reaction. He stopped at me.

'Doonan! Stop flinching! Venereal disease does not discriminate. Even monarchs get the pox, you know!'

This was the kind of alarming titbit that the teachers and radio broadcasters of yore kept up their sleeves to enliven the dryness of history. They were no fools. These educators knew that, without the occasional bonbon of scandal, their lessons were nothing more than sleep-induction devices. As a result, everyone in England knows all kinds of appalling things about the European monarchs.

Every schoolchild knows that Edward II died after his tormentors shoved a hot poker up his bottie, and that Catherine the Great regularly succumbed to unsavoury interspecies cravings involving geese. And Louis XIV suffered from anal fistulas, and last, Henry VIII rotted away from syphilis.

I was fascinated and appalled by this mysterious and shameful ailment. I read anything and everything about the symptoms and the dreadful things that happened if syphilis went untreated. There were sores and pustules in horrible, inopportune places, and then the nerves in your feet rotted and you started to walk like Herman Munster. And more often than not your nose rotted and caved in. By this time your willie would also have dropped off.

Then, when you could no longer walk and your nose and your willie were in a medical-waste bin at the far end of the hospital car park, madness would set in. This was followed by a horrible, lingering death, after which you were *no longer with us*.

I inhaled all these details, little knowing that I was already afflicted.

The Saturday morning of my diagnosis was no different from any other. There I was, curled up on the floor in front of the fire, flicking petulantly through a ladies' magazine while the rain pounded on the windows. I was irate because, yet again, I was wearing my school uniform on the weekend. I had recently become aware that not every child wore a school uniform seven days a week. Some children – *most children!* – had *clothes*! My parents – even my vain and stylish mother – seemed oblivious to the concept of sportswear or leisure wear for kids, and I, with my burgeoning interest in fashion, had had enough of my green and grey uniform.

I tired of looking at the fashions and turned to the horoscope page.

I should explain that, despite the astrological branch in our family tree, my parents never set much store by horoscopes, deeming them to be 'a load of cobblers'. They practised no formal religion. Like the existentialists, whose philosophy was so madly au courant at the time, Betty and Terry saw life as a chaotic, random experience.

They were, if you will, the Jean-Paul and Simone of our neighbourhood.

So there I was reading my own horoscope in my grey flannel shorts and strangling tie, and wondering why people actually believed in such things. My star sign, Scorpio, contained the usual cliché advice about 'matters of the heart' and vague chidings about the optimal times for undertaking journeys and home improvements.

Then, out of the blue, came a surprisingly sinister warning.

Scorpios, so said this particular astrologer, must be vigilant about their health. They were prone to die from ailments that afflicted the bowels and genitals.

Bingo!

Suddenly everything fell into place. I was a Scorpio. I had bowels and genitals. Syphilis was a disease that afflicted those nether regions. Voilà!

I understood that sex was a key factor in the transmission of syphilis. I was no fool. Not like my Irish grandpa.

'For God's sakes, whatever you do, don't be wearin' other people's shoes. You'll catch the pox, sure ya will!'

Poor old bloke! He actually thought you could catch it from wearing other people's shoes. Even back then, I knew this was silly. Anybody could see that, at the very least, one would have to have sex with another person's shoes in order to catch their pox. It was clearly not *just* about wearing them.

Regarding Sex. I was already an enthusiast, albeit of the frustrated variety. I was dying to kiss and cuddle with somebody, anybody, but preferably one of the cowboys on *Laramie*. I was also willing to be on intimate terms with Illya Kuryakin on *The Man from U.N.C.L.E.*, Dick Van Dyke, Sean Connery and James Dean.

I would also have kissed any of the blokes on 77 *Sunset Strip* (including the father), the elder brother in *Flipper*, ditto *My Three Sons*. I was ten and hormone-riddled and would have happily gone on dates with any of the above. I even fancied Chester, the limping sheriff on *Gunsmoke*.

Various boring legal, logistical and geographical stumbling blocks prevented these liaisons from ever taking place. As a result I had no outlet for my desires. All that libidinal energy roiled and boiled inside my green braid-trimmed school blazer. Here it accumulated and festered, aided by a growing sense that my particular brand of love was taboo. Gradually my transgressive longings morphed into some horrible sense that I had already committed an appalling sin of some kind. I had somehow done something nasty with someone who was also quite nasty.

And this unknown incubus had given me a raging case of the pox.

I was already displaying symptoms. There were spots on my willie. They were very faint, but I was convinced I could see them. Any mention of venereal disease on radio or TV would send me scampering to the toilet to examine my blighted regions. The subject seemed to come up with amazing and inconvenient frequency. I was constantly in the bathroom examining my various areas. Compulsive hand washing ensued.

I couldn't tell anyone about my affliction. I knew enough to understand that my fall from grace would bring shame on the whole family. I would probably be sent away like the poor teenage girls in our town who got themselves knocked up and then had to go and live with relatives in other towns and spend the rest of their lives pretending to be the elder sisters of their own children.

There was only one option open to me. I would have to cure myself.

From Buckingham Palace to Coronation Street, every English home has one great common denominator. There is always a bottle of Harpic next to the toilet. The sight of that blue-and-white chequered bottle nestling insouciantly next to the plunger is as much part of British life as bangers 'n' mash.

Here, in this bottle, was the answer to all my problems.

'HARPIC – kills all known germs. Dead!'

The text on the bottle did not mention anything about curing syphilis, but that emphatic slogan – 'HARPIC – kills all known germs. Dead!' – left me in no doubt that it could, and would.

Sunday night was bath night. Yes, dear reader, we bathed only once a week. Please don't reproach me or look down your nose. We were not unusual in this regard.

Weekly baths were the norm, even into the 1960s. Many families even dunked their kids in the same water, *à la* sheep dip.

I wish I could defend this practice and direct your attentions to some fabulous upside to this grim tradition. I wish I could claim that, as result of minimal contact with soap and water, we all had dewy, translucent skin or silky hair. But we didn't. Our skin and hair were OK but nothing special. The fact is that three baths a week would have been preferable.

Back to my willie.

As bath night approached, I prepared for my cure with anxious excitement. I made sure we were well stocked with Harpic.

'Don't forget to wash behind your ears!' yelled Betty as I locked the door and braced myself for what would no doubt be a historic ablution.

Based on the shrill warnings on the side of the bottle, I assumed the treatment might cause a little discomfort. I was tough. I was Betty's son. I could handle it.

After going through my regular toilette, I readied myself. Kneeling in the soapy, lukewarm water, I unscrewed the top of the Harpic bottle. It all seemed rather baptismal. I smiled a beatific smile.

Slowly and deliberately, I poured the white liquid on my afflicted parts and braced myself. At first it felt cool and vaguely refreshing. Then my willie began to tingle. Within seconds, the tingling turned to fire and the fire to searing agony. I fell backwards into the bath, sending a mini tsunami of soapy water over the side.

Automatically, my body began to arch upwards. Very soon only the back of my head and my heels were touching the bath, such was the pain. I caught sight of myself in the steamy bathroom tiles. I looked like a tortured pink fleshy version of the Sydney Harbour Bridge.

Surprisingly, the pain actually increased. I chomped on a loofah to stop myself screaming the house down and began to count to ten. One . . . two . . . three . . . This would give the Harpic – four . . . five . . . six – the time it needed to kill all known germs . . . seven . . . eight . . . nine . . . 10 . . . *dead*!

Cure complete, I doused my willie under the cold tap and collapsed in a relieved and happy heap on the bathroom floor. I was saved!

Still gasping, I thought of all the sinners over all the centuries who had, pre-Harpic, died in their vermin-ridden hovels and gave thanks.

If only Henry VIII had had access to a bottle or two of Harpic, I mused to myself as I extracted loofah fronds from my teeth, it might have changed the course of history.

Yes, there was a little blistering, but at least I no longer had venereal disease. I wasn't going to die, at least not now.

~

The next assault on my nether regions occurred five years later.

When I was 15 a pea-sized stone made its way from my kidney to my bladder. I was watching TV at the time. The pain was indescribable. I went very white and collapsed on the floor. I dug my fingers into the handmade fireside rug, which schizophrenic Uncle Ken had hooked during one of his occupational therapy frenzies.

Betty encouraged the rug making. It was infinitely preferable to the basket-making period which had preceded it. There was nothing aesthetically wrong with the trays and wastebaskets Ken produced with such relentless ardour. They were, in fact, quite lovely. It was the endless soaking of endless bales of wicker which occupied the bathtub for days at a time and interfered with the beauty routines of the more glam members of our household.

Gradually the agony subsided. I assumed a casual position on Ken's rug – lying on my front with my legs kicking back and forth at the knee – and continued watching *Laramie*.

Anyone Jewish who is reading this will wonder why I did not call out to my parents and demand that a helicopter transport me to the nearest hospital. This is an entirely valid question. All I can tell you, by way of explanation, is that Gentiles are different. We use our stiff upper lips and our innate indifference as a shield against reality – i.e. we're insane.

Later that evening, the aforementioned kidney stone, along with a great deal of blood and human tissue, embarked on the second leg of its journey. The pain was far worse than anything I experienced on Ken's rug or during my syphilis cure. My nether regions were literally vibrating with agony. I decamped to the bathroom and thought about the dire predictions in that long-lost horoscope.

The evil stone travelled slowly, very slowly, from my bladder down the length of my willie. At last, pea-sized and bloody, it greeted the outside world and plopped into the toilet.

I was now ready to break the Gentile conspiracy of silence.

I wrapped toilet paper around my private parts and staggered downstairs. Gingerly opening the living room door, I asked, very formally, to speak to Terry. He followed me back upstairs. I tried to explain what had happened and pointed at the gore which glistened in the toilet bowl.

'We should probably take the stone to the doctor. He will doubtless want to take it to his laboratory and analyse it,' I said, assuming that, as my parent, he should be the one to reach in and fish for it.

'Oh, no,' said Terry, with the air of a father who thinks his son might be developing delusions of grandeur. 'The doctor won't be interested.' With that, he flushed the toilet and made me a cup of tea.

Three days later we paid a visit to the doctor.

Again, all I can tell you by way of explanation, is that we Gentiles feel that rushing to the hospital emergency room is a sign of extreme hysteria.

'Well, I certainly hope you kept the stone so that we can analyse it in our laboratory,' said the doctor, who like many of his profession at the time, smoked cigarettes during consultations.

'*He* flushed it,' I said, glaring at Terry.

'Since you did not have the presence of mind to keep the stone' – puff, puff, glare, glare – 'I have no way of knowing what caused it. The only advice I can give you is to drink lots of rhubarb juice. Next patient!'

Terry lived to regret his parental laissez-faire. Even when he was in his 80s, I still took pleasure in reminding him of his role Kidney-gate.

'Have some more rhubarb juice,' was his usual reply.

A furious gust of wind enters the room and blows the pages of the calendar forwards, ever forwards. Seasons come and go. Hairdos change. Gauchos come and go, as do culottes. The pages eventually stop turning.

It's 1977. The year that Elvis died. I am 25 years old. The siege of the nether regions continues unabated.

I am standing, legs spread, in the show window of City à la Mode.

This store serves the needs of secretaries in the financial district of London. Serviceable, staid fashions are sold upstairs, while lingerie, foundation garments, stockings, and tights are sold downstairs. At lunchtime the store is overrun with shrieking office girls buying essential and non-essential garments. The rest of the day is quiet.

The sales staff of City à la Mode alleviated the tedium by feuding with each other. The upstairs ladies directed a white-hot hatred towards the basement ladies and vice versa. I have no idea why. When shipments of panties and brassieres arrived, the upstairs ladies would hurl the boxes downstairs without any warning. Bundles of hard plastic hangers were also used as missiles. Nobody seemed able to remember what had started this conflict. It was just one of those nasty tribal things. Whenever I read about massacres like the one in Rwanda, I always think of the ladies of City à la Mode.

I was a freelance window dresser, appearing once a week on this battlefield and vastly relieved not to be involved. From my vantage point in the store window, it was all very entertaining.

My main responsibility was to change the merchandise in the show windows. This is more complex than might ever be imagined. To strip and redress a mannequin, it is first necessary to remove the wig, especially if the wig is large. My City à la Mode wigs were not large. They were gigantic. No muumuu, no matter how enormous, would ever fit over them. These massive, lacquered, crinkly confections were styled in a manner that is now associated with cheap girls from New Jersey (think Joan Cusack in *Working Girl*) but was new and groovy at the time of the incident.

Wig removal, though not brain surgery, was no mean feat. Two sturdy steel pins anchored the wig to the mannequin's head. These pins slid into two dense cork inserts, which were embedded in either temple. The pins were extracted with pliers and reinserted with the aid of a small hammer. Every time I reattached the wigs, hammering the two-inch pin into the mannequin skull, I thought of Narg and her lobotomy.

The wigs were by no means the most complex part of the procedure. Changing the tights presented the biggest challenge. The fibreglass legs could not be brought together with the ease of human legs. A tremendous amount of strenuous yanking and stretching was required. Before one could even begin to remove the old pair, the mannequin in question had to be lifted from her baseplate. Screwed into that baseplate was a seven-inch rod. This rod disappeared into the foot and stabilised the mannequin. These projectiles are the bane of a window dresser's existence because they are always getting lodged inside the feet.

When dogs are stuck together a bucket of cold water will often effect a separation. With mannequins there is no such miracle cure. One has to grab the girl under the crotch and pull her in a vertically upwards direction.

It helps to be tall. I'm not.

I had been struggling with one particular mannequin, much to the amusement of passers-by, for about ten minutes. Frustration set in. I decided to employ brute force. I grabbed and yanked with all my window dresser's might.

Twang!

A nasty, painful sensation clutched at the right side of my groin. I had popped a hernia.

Three months later, after wading through the NHS bureaucracy, I was admitted to hospital. In preparation for the operation, I was wheeled into a tiny room by a rather suspect old geezer whose job it was to shave male patients before surgery.

'I like a lad with smooth skin,' he said with a friendly leer. 'So much nicer than those half-witted tarts you see dancing about on the telly.'

He took a keen interest in his métier. In fact, I cannot recall ever seeing anyone enjoy his occupation more. Here was somebody whose job fit him like a glove.

There would have been no point in complaining about the old fellah and getting him fired. The hospital human resources department would then have had to undertake the momentous task of finding someone who was willing to spend his days removing hair from an assortment of nether regions. Given the unappetising nature of the work, it seemed best left to someone who had a special interest.

After the operation, I was placed in an open ward with

about 45 fellow post-operatives. Many had undergone leg amputation as a result of diabetes and thrombosis, and were being driven crazy by phantom limb pain and itchy stumps. I was in this ward for an insanely boring ten days and passed the time chatting to these Long John Silvers, lighting their cigarettes, and obligingly scratching their stumps with a cane back scratcher.

The surgeon came by one day and found me pushing one of my new wheelchair-bound friends – an ancient working-class gentleman with no teeth and droll wit – round the ward *à la* Grand Prix. Our jolly jape occasioned a public reprimand.

'You'd better be bloody careful, young man,' said the outraged doctor, addressing me. 'I sewed plastic mesh into the wall of your groin to hold your guts in place. If you exert yourself, you will sieve your own intestines and make them into foie gras!' With a bang of a rubber door, he was gone.

'Oooh! If it's not one thing it's another,' said my fellow patient, and we returned sheepishly to our respective beds.

It's been a while since anything nasty happened *down there*. Rest assured, the minute any fresh catastrophe afflicts my nether regions and threatens my mortality, you will be the first to know.

Chapter 15

HOLLYWOOD

MY HOLLYWOOD years were encrusted with a sparkly combo of tawdriness and tinsel.

In 1980 I moved into an apartment building in Hollywood, California, called the Fontenoy. This French chateâu-style structure was drenched with poorly researched movie-star lore. An older resident started the whole thing by claiming that Marilyn Monroe had once lived on the sixth floor, sharing an apartment and many lipsticks and stiletto heels with Shelley Winters.

Not to be outdone, we new tenants all made stories up about our various apartments.

'Did you know that Cyd Charisse once tried to jump out of the window of my apartment? You can see her heel marks on the window sill.'

'That's nothing. Apparently Robert Mitchum used to live in my apartment. He left all his TV dinners in the freezer.'

Looking at the dusty raggle-taggle of human flotsam who now occupied the cockroach-infested apartments, it was hard to imagine the former glory days of the Fontenoy. The only celeb resident during my tenure was Nicolas Cage, who wasn't a celeb at the time, just an affable, thick-haired ingénue.

The dearth of celebs in no way diminishes the fondness I feel for my Hollywood years. I have nothing but warm, fuzzy, nostalgic feelings for my old neighbourhood, and with good reason. The Fontenoy was just up the street from Frederick's of Hollywood and the magical sleaze of Hollywood Boulevard. Most of the local shops, taking their cue from Frederick's, sold stripper clothing, high-heeled shoes and theatrical wigs. If you wanted ordinary groceries, you had to drive miles to a supermarket. If you wanted edible panties, Frederick's was a two-minute stroll past the transvestite prostitutes who worked the intersection of Yucca and Whitley streets in *Flashdance* T-shirts, acid-washed jeans, and pearlised scrunch boots.

Also within walking distance were the Max Factor Museum, which boasted a beauty calibrating machine; the

Scientology Center, which did not yet boast Tom Cruise; the Hollywood Wax Museum; and a home for teenage runaways called Hudson House. With my predilection for everything camp and/or grotesque, this location suited me down to the ground. I could pop out and look at the stars embedded in the pavement on Hollywood Boulevard any time of the day or night – 'Look, there's Pat Boone! There's Phyllis Diller!' Living at the Fontenoy was like being at a Butlins Holiday Camp all year round.

The neighbourhood boasted several Butlinesque themed eateries.

Top of the list was a 'family restaurant' called The Tick-Tock. The walls of The Tick-Tock were covered with ticking and gonging clocks of all varieties, a cruel reminder to the mostly older patrons of the fact that they would soon be *no longer with us*.

It was here among the cuckoo and carriage clocks that I witnessed my very first Heimlich manoeuvre. A glamorous senior citizen in a turban – a Gloria Swanson manqué – suddenly clutched her throat with both hands and began to make choking noises.

'Aiiieeyye! Madre de Diós! She shokin'!' screamed a sturdy Mexican waitress.

The observant Latina then tangoed the patron from her banquette. Her movements seemed well-practiced. She grabbed the distressed senior around the middle and, with vigorous upwards hugging motions, dislodged half a semi-masticated dinner roll from her trachea. The blockage hit the floor with a light *splat*. A round of applause followed. The hungry patron returned to her tuna melt. She left a big tip.

Other Hollywood residents were less fortunate. Horrid gangs would take drive-by potshots at the local trannies. On more than one occasion we saw a large, ungainly she-male crumple to the pavement and lie motionless.

There was drama on every corner.

One night some of the Hudson boys decided, somewhat rashly, to torch their home. Like rioters who ravage their own neighbourhood, these hoodlums were experiencing that strange, primordial impulse to shoot oneself in the foot. We watched from our seventh-floor window as the homeless lads poured lighter fluid on their nicely renovated house, funded probably by charitable contributions from someone like Jerry Lewis or Barbra Streisand, and then danced jubilantly round the burning building. This was the equivalent of inmates in a battered women's shelter deciding to batter themselves. The next day the homeless boys sat staring at the charred debris looking surprised and annoyed, as if wondering who had done the damage.

I shared my Fontenoy years with a person called Mundo. A painter and a window dresser, Mundo was soulful, humble and unique. He was in his early 20s. We were in love in the insane, thoughtless way that afflicts the young, which sounds like a cliché out of a cheesy romance novel but is nonetheless quite accurate. After two tumultuous years, our relationship morphed, much to our mutual relief, into a loving friendship.

We had a great deal in common. We were first-generation immigrants in the land of opportunity. For us this represented an opportunity to have oodles of fun and spend a great deal of time mocking each other's ethnicity while also being fascinated by it. I was intrigued by his Mexicanness, he was enthralled by everything that was trendy and English. He introduced me to Frida Kahlo paintings and *ranchera* music; I introduced him to Boy George acolytes like Pinkietessa Braithwaite and the pop star Marilyn. They had recently moved from London and lived just around the corner.

For Mundo and me, being trendy was our most intense and satisfying area of commonality. I had long since given up trying to find the Beautiful People. The few rich international types that I had met, especially the European ones, all seemed irredeemably naff and hopelessly self-obsessed. Yes, they wore caftans, but what, in 1980, could be more out of date? They spent their days dabbling in various forms of spirituality and experimenting with new beauty treatments. Most damning of all, these BP's all seemed to have the same lousy sense of humour: in the world of the Beautiful People, accidentally dropping a teaspoon on the floor, missing a plane, or forgetting to wind your watch all seem to qualify as riotously funny, thigh-slapping occurrences.

If you are gorgeous and wealthy, you lack the motivation to develop a great wit. If you are a marginalised freak like me or Marilyn or Pinkie, a caustic tongue is a pre-requisite for attention if not survival.

I now settled happily for the trendy people, not because they were fashionable but because they were wicked and funny and irreverent.

There was no shortage of activities for us marginalised trendoids in Hollywood. This was the early 80s, when, if you were au courant, you were probably worshiping ABC, Bow Wow Wow, and the Thompson Twins. Every week another new band of hopefuls – Spandau Ballet, Madness, the Specials, Siouxsie Sioux – was playing at the Roxy or the Whiskey a Go-Go. My clearest memory from this period is watching Nina Hagen perform dressed as a nun. After a couple of numbers she turned around, revealing a lifelike black rubber phallus sticking, at a 45 degree angle, through the folds of her habit. Bon appétit!

When we weren't watching live music, Mundo and I were flitting about in Vivienne Westwood pirate gear at 'New Romantic' clubs with names like The Veil, The Fake, and Club Lingerie. It was good, old-fashioned, pointless fun. We took full advantage of the vogue for costumey dress-up. I have boxes of snaps of us in various guises: Mundo dressed as Valentino; me as Betty Rubble, Mundo as a goat-legged Bacchus; and me as Queen Elizabeth II. I am probably the only white male on the planet who has ever cross-dressed as the African songstress Miriam Makeba. The apotheosis of our overdressed trendiness occurred when we were recruited for the Kim Carnes 'Bette Davis Eyes' video. That's my gloved hand in the opening shot.

Don't judge me too harshly: if you're not going to be a trendy, superficial poseur in your 20s, when *are* you going to do it?

We supported ourselves and our habits with money made from installing display windows in shops around town. Despite the foofy nature of our social life, Mundo and I took our work very seriously. We prided ourselves on our familiarity with the prop rental houses that dotted Los Angeles. Here lurked the surreal follies which were the very nuts and bolts of the movie industry. These included, but were not limited to, terrifying oversized carnival heads, stuffed rattlesnakes, fake scenic rocks on wheels, charging bulls on wheels, alert collie dogs and limp hit-by-a-car collie dogs, life-sized anatomy dolls, and fake salamis and cheeses of every size and description. Our favourite trick was to locate something impossibly grotesque and then see if we could seamlessly integrate it into the display window of a fancy Beverly Hills luxury goods store.

When I met Mundo, I was already known for my outré displays at a store called Maxfield Bleu. I had evolved considerably from the pedestrian fashion vignettes of my City à la Mode days. My windows now regularly included such things as coffins, suicides and mannequins juggling taxidermied cats.

Mundo came along and made me look like a light-weight. His window displays – in sharp contrast to his mild manner – were completely insane. He was, for some reason, infinitely less risk-averse than even I. This may have been due to the fact that I had a green card and he did not; i.e. he had nothing to lose.

Together we reached new heights of provocation. One of the windows for which I am best known, a vignette inspired by a local news item, depicting the abduction of a newborn baby by a vicious coyote from a suburban home, was one such collaboration. After complaints from individuals claiming kin with the abductee, we removed the window.

When we worked together, I was a moderating influence. When Mundo went off on his own, he really went over the top. One day I stopped by a store where he was working to see what he was up to. Even I was taken aback. Somewhere in the bowels of some far-flung studio prop rental warehouse, he had managed to find a series of stuffed warthog heads. He had mounted them on large, shocking pink plywood panels and juxtaposed them next to fluorescent-hued Norma Kamali dresses. I arrived just in time to see the apoplectic store owner gesticulating wildly in front of the window, while an oblivious Mundo – a can of hairspray in one hand and a ratting comb in the other – lovingly coiffed the tufty heads of his warthogs.

His ideas were very proto-Damien Hirst. Unlike Mr Hirst and many of the new post-skill artists of today, Mundo was an accomplished painter. He used this skill to earn extra money, painting commissioned portraits.

Having no such talents, I augmented my window-dressing earnings with a T-shirt business. I silk-screened and hand-painted garments with designs of my own making and sold them to Melrose Avenue stores. When I needed a bit of extra cash, I would park on a side street, near my retailers, and sell them out of the back of my truck. This guerrilla salesmanship often yielded as much as five hundred dollars on a busy Saturday, which seemed like a fortune at the time.

As I look back on this entrepreneurial, skip-along period of my life, I realise what a huge role my T-shirt business played in all aspects of my personal growth. The organisational and interpersonal skills I acquired, through trial and error, transformed me into a fully functional human being. I'm not joking. I have absolutely no idea why people bother going to fancy colleges: everything you will ever need to know about life and more can be learned through the operation of a T-shirt business.

Example: the first time I delivered a bunch of T-shirts to a store, I shipped them out with an invoice tucked neatly inside the package. I felt very efficient and businesslike. When, 30 days later, I had received no payment, I became irate. I called the accounts office.

'Oh, you must be the brain surgeon who sent an invoice without a return address. Honey, your cheque is sitting right here. You do know what a cheque is, don'tcha, honey?'

I genuinely feel that prior to operating a T-shirt business I was a mentally subnormal, incompetent, trend-obsessed fool. And after three years in the T-shirt business, I became – without a hint of exaggeration – a world-class sage.

One day Mundo stopped by the studio where I silk-screened my garments. We chatted. He smoked a joint. Before leaving, he showed me a purple lump on his neck and asked me for a diagnosis.

'It's just an ingrowing hair,' I said, instinctively playing it down and thereby doing a total Terry Doonan.

A couple of weeks later Mundo and I and a couple of friends, including his current boyfriend, Jef, were lolling round our glamorous oval-shaped pool. It was an evening of giggling and synchronised swimming and cocktails with little umbrellas in them.

'A woman in the elevator told me Lana Turner once cracked her head on the bottom of this pool,' said Mundo, looking like a young Xavier Cugat in his vintage resort shirt and straw hat.

We all got fairly plastered and started making glamorous Lana Turner head-injury turbans out of our towels, climbing the palm trees and taking snaps of each other.

I still have those photographs. When I look at them I think, These were taken the night before our happy, silly, trendy Hollywood lives changed so irrevocably and horribly.

The next day.

Hungover and exhausted from the previous night's capers, I came home early from work. I found Mundo sitting on the couch, staring out at the Capitol Records tower. He looked puffy-eyed.

'Are you high? You lazy Mexicans and your pot!' I mocked affectionately. (I always think the real purpose of a relationship is to provide a 'safe space' for the voicing of such un-PC thoughts.)

He did not laugh. He kept on staring at Capitol Records.

'The doctor says it's cancer. I have AIDS.'

I screamed. I did not cry tears. I just let out this weird, womanly wail. Over the next few months Mundo would try to imitate the noise I had made. He would laugh and tell me how like an outraged English matron I had sounded.

These were early days in the history of the Plague. I had heard about AIDS. I had read the landmark *Village Voice* piece a few months before. I assumed this disease was something that afflicted the sexual outlaws of West Hollywood, Castro Street and Greenwich Village, where excessive practices had somehow created a new affliction. I never imagined it could strike someone who did things like dressing up as a Fellini clown or buying Mexican pastries and then spending all weekend painting gorgeous

still lifes of them while listening to his parents' old La
Lupe records.

After I let out my Lady Bracknell scream, I panicked.
Then I got mad.

'This doctor is obviously a lunatic!' I said, channelling
my inner Betty Doonan. 'I will personally make sure he is
struck off the register for misdiagnosing people and
giving them nervous breakdowns.'

We would show him!

I badly needed to persuade myself that we had been
the victims of some kind of hoax. The insidious nature of
AIDS, with its long gestation period, meant that Mundo's
diagnosis was my diagnosis. Maybe I had given it to him
or he to me. Who knows? Either way, we were all
doomed. In the back of my mind I realised that the
dreaded Scorpio horoscope had come to pass. Though
AIDS was not technically a disease of the nether regions,
it seemed to fit the bill.

A week later I accompanied Mundo to get the results
of his biopsy. I had moved out of denial mode into a
permanently nauseated mode. While I sat pretending to
read magazines and trying not to vomit into the snake
plants, I observed the other people in the waiting room.
One in particular sticks in my memory. He was a middle-
aged man with an enormous amount of bleached hair. It
was a horrid, brassy-greeny-blond colour, exactly the
shade against which my mother had inveighed for so
many years. With great skill he had combed and swirled

his tresses around various parts of his face in order to hide the lumpy purple lesions that afflicted him. His hair was yellow and his sweater was yellow and his face was violet-coloured. His terrified, depressed eyes peered through the swirls of hair.

Mundo came out of the doctor's office looking bleak. The biopsy had confirmed that his skin lesions were Kaposi's sarcoma. The doctor told him there was nothing he could do for him. AIDS was a terminal illness.

Being cut loose from the medical profession produced a very strange free-falling sensation. We did not quite know what to do next. When your cure is left up to you, you don't know whether to run into the woods and start looking for healing berries or jump out of the window of your apartment. AIDS was clearly beyond the scope of Harpic.

Feeling decidedly unhinged, I drove Mundo to the health-food store in West Hollywood. It was called Erehwon, which is *nowhere* spelled backward, which is precisely where we were.

Still channelling Betty, I raged through the store, buying sacks of wheat germ and nuts and brewer's yeast. Betty was a health-food devotee, as was Aunt Phyllis. We regularly ate nut cutlets and home-grown bean shoots. Betty was, like the overdressed romance novelist Barbara Cartland, a believer in the mystical powers of organic honey. I picked up a couple of vats for good measure. Mundo was starting to look at me as if I had gone bonkers, which of course I very nearly had.

On the bulletin board of the health-food store, I saw something that caught my eye. It was a notice advertising a macrobiotic healing centre. I let out another womanly shriek. The macro flyer claimed success treating people with AIDS!!!!

I drove home at about 90 miles an hour and called. Before you could screech 'tofu stroganoff!' we were both having macrobiotic cooking lessons and chomping on chunks of seaweed. Though not the trendiest, most amusing people on Earth, the crunchy hippies at the East-West Center were, unlike Mundo's doctor, full of hope and encouragement. Here Mundo read all about the macro founder George Ohsawa's triumph over tuberculosis. He even had a consultation with the grand macro poobah, a bloke called Michio Kushi, who put him on a rigorously ascetic diet.

Meanwhile, Mundo's mother was doing her bit. She was non-judgemental, kind and quite eccentric. In predominantly Mexican East LA, Mundo's mamacita was known as something of a local healer, a woman with special powers. At all hours of the day and night, the locals picked their way through the gnomes on her front lawn seeking advice and herbal remedies.

She prescribed for Mundo an ancient regimen of healing rituals. He boiled handfuls of strange herbs in cauldrons of water. He was then obliged to sleep with a bowl of herb-infused water under his bed and a glass of the same water on a shelf over his bed. In the morning he had to drink the water over his head and toss out the water under his bed. He did this religiously for months.

While this hocus-pocus seemed to have a positive effect on Mundo, the same could not be said for his diet. The whole macro thing was, in retrospect, not such a great idea. The switch from the fatty, meaty Latin American diet to a Japanese regimen caused Mundo to lose loads of weight quite rapidly. He was skinny to begin with. As his body weight dropped, the lesions proliferated. One night at the movies he showed me a lesion which he was convinced had appeared during the previews.

Any time he went to get help from Social Security, he was treated like a leper. This was before Rock Hudson or Freddie Mercury or Liz Taylor's fund-raisers. The official Ronald Reagan attitude at this time was that a small number of gay men had contracted this self-inflicted disease because of their disgusting practices and that they should go away and die before infecting anyone else. In fairness to Ronald and Nancy, this was also my attitude and that of many gay men before coming into direct contact with the disease.

And what of Mundo? you are no doubt wondering. How was he coping? *Magically* is the word that springs to mind. He was calm and dignified and barely 25 years old. Despite the physical disintegration, the lack of money and medical support, he never complained. He cooked his grains and braised his tempeh, painted, watched movies, and scoured the Goodwill for modernist furniture. He and his boyfriend, Jef, fought and made love like a regular couple.

I, meanwhile, was lonely, grief-stricken, and prone to bouts of hysteria. I thought about death and disease 24 hours a day.

After two years of relatively good health, Mundo started to deteriorate. His lesions became horribly disfiguring. 'I'm turning into the Elephant Man,' he said, not without a certain amount of accuracy.

Mundo got sick of trying to explain his ghastly affliction to probing friends and neighbours. He and his devoted Jef moved to the other side of the railway tracks, near Glendale.

One night I descended on him to take him out for dinner. It was his birthday. Jef was out of town. He asked me to bring a tin of Pan-Cake make-up. Painstakingly, he sponged it on, covering his swollen face and his lesions. Before he got dressed, I gave him his birthday present. It was a trendy and not inexpensive outfit by a Japanese designer. Having just finished working on the movie *Beverly Hills Cop,* where I designed the notorious gallery scene, I was flush with cash. My generosity was motivated by guilt: I felt bad that Mundo was missing out on these fun jobs which had come my way as a result of our window collaborations.

Our date was surreal. The maquillaged, emaciated Mundo somehow looked even stranger than usual, like an alien with a beige apple head and a limp rag-doll body. We drove far into the San Fernando Valley and found a frou-frou French restaurant where we had a candlelit dinner. His ability to enjoy silly, simple things was completely undiminished. Even though he had lesions on his feet, which necessitated the wearing of huge sheepskin scuffies, he insisted on going out dancing. We asked the obviously gay waiter to recommend a local hot spot. After dinner we drove to a turgid disco called Angles or Spangles or something like that. We began to dance. Before the end of the first song, Mundo's insane appearance had virtually cleared the dance floor. He laughed about the way he looked and at people's horrified reactions. It was like a horrible, negative version of that scenario where Fred and Ginger clear the floor with their expertise. We did it with a disease.

'Thanks for the great birthday!' he said, without any trace of cynicism, when I dropped him off.

Mundo was much better at dying than I was at watching him die.

The last two months of his life were like watching a crucifixion. His lungs would fill up with water every couple of days. The doctor would draw out the fluid with a long needle, while Mundo was fully conscious, filling massive surgical bottles. He never complained.

Between agonizing procedures, he would demand to be driven to the Beverly Center where, for some unknown reason, he insisted on buying toy Godzillas in various sizes. This remarkable impulse demonstrated, more than anything else I have ever witnessed, the magical, life-affirming power of *shopping*. Long after his appetite for television or food or music evaporated, Mundo retained the impulse to shop for a Godzilla or even a pack of tube socks.

Soon his condition worsened and he became bedridden. There were no more trips to the Beverly Center.

While everything I ever learned about the practicalities of Life came from my T-shirt business, everything I have learned about death and dying came from Mundo.

Before Mundo's demise, I had no deathbed skills whatsoever. I cringe when I recall my silly bedside manner. My first impulse was to try to compensate for the dire situation by talking too much, acting in an animated and 'hilarious' fashion, and bringing him snuggly toys and other irritating crap, which clogged his hospital room. I was like a manic version of Shari Lewis, minus Lamb Chop.

One day a chatty nurse in white clogs dropped by to draw blood.

'Hi, hon. My feet are killing me. I had to park miles away. No room because of the blood drive,' she said, indicating the large tent set up in the car park where conscientious citizens were donating their pints.

'I think I'll stop by on the way out,' I said, hoping to sound worthy and upstanding.

'No offence, sugar-dumplin', but I don't think anyone wants your blood,' she said and busied herself with Mundo's chart.

This blunt, Nargesque comment caused me to become a little teary and histrionic. Mundo glared at me through the swollen purple hell that was formerly his lovely handsome face.

'Calm down, daughter!' (Naturally, I had taught him to *daughter!*)

He sighed and patted me on the head. 'Why can't you be like Rudi?'

Rudi was my new Japanese housemate. I do not mean to imply that I had a series of Japanese housemates. Rudi was my new housemate who *happened to be* Japanese. We were sisters.

When Rudi came to visit Mundo, he would serve him take-out sushi from the restaurant where he worked. Then, for the next half hour, he would sit as still and quiet as a waiting geisha. Considering the lack of sizzling banter, I was surprised by how much Mundo looked forward to Rudi's visits.

The next time I went to see Mundo I tried the Rudi technique.

I walked quietly into the room and gave Mundo a quick hug. I then sat down and said nothing.

This proved to be far more difficult than my previous jabbering and mugging. I went through several stages of social discomfort and panic. The clock ticked. Mundo wheezed. Embarrassing moments passed.

Gradually I got used to the quiet. Slowly, very slowly, I lost track of time. A nurse came and went. Mundo dozed. The clock ticked. Mundo woke up.

He finally broke the silence.

'There are crowds of people waiting for me,' he said, staring straight ahead.

'There are?' I said, mystified. 'What do they look like?'

'They are Indians,' replied Mundo, who had a distinctly pre-Columbian look about him. He was proud of his Tarahumara Indian roots and often, especially after a couple of joints, painted pictures of haunting Aztec-looking dudes.

There was a long pause, during which I reflected on how godless I was and how lucky Mundo was to actually believe in something.

'They are weaving a banner.'

'What kind of banner?'

'It's a welcome banner.'

'Oh.'

'As soon as the banner is finished, I am going to join them.'

Two days later he went into a coma. Then, on 11 February, 1985, Mundo went to join his new friends.

Chapter 16

CREVICE NOZZLES

J UST call me Dora Doom.

I never expected that I would survive the Plague. I spent most of the 1980s going to memorials and waiting to be struck down. This was a dark and horrid time. Loony obsessions dominated my thoughts. It was impossible for me to look at my skin without seeing the shadowy beginnings of a deadly cancerous lesion. When I tested negative for HIV, I was convinced that it was a mistake and that I would still get sick.

And then I didn't die. I survived.

My survival is not the result of anything other than the

fact that I'm a prissy sissy. My prissiness saved my life. With my germ phobia and a smidgen of good luck, I eluded death.

Being of a fastidious disposition, I always felt disinclined to engage in those *practices* which increase the likelihood of contamination of any kind. (My prissiness also disinclines me from describing these *practices* in detail, but I feel sure you have a rough idea what I'm talking about.)

I have spent many years in psychotherapy discussing my germ phobia and general, all-around pernicketyness. From what I can gather, I have Narg and Uncle Ken to thank. Growing up with lunatics tends, so I am told, to imbue children with a fear of contamination, both physiological and psychological. Now, as I look back on the devastation caused by AIDS and on the long list of lost friends and acquaintances, I have ceased to regard my prissiness as a problem. Though prissiness in and of itself did not save my life, it clearly decreased the probabilities in my favour. It has definitely proven itself to be more of a lifesaver than a disadvantage.

Thanks, Narg. Thanks, Uncle Ken.

In addition to my priss factor, I must also acknowledge my fear of, dare I say it, penetration. This particular fixation has, for reasons that are too obvious to require explanation, clearly played an additional role in my survival.

The blame for my fear of penetration cannot be laid at Narg and Ken's door.

It all goes back to a horrid Freudian trauma which occurred in the early 1960s. Like so many Freudian traumas, it involved horses.

Betty Doonan's parenting was not heavily focused on education. Having left school at the age of 13 and successfully clawed her way to the middle, or at least the lower half of it, she was not overly fixated on academic achievement.

The most important thing, as far as Betty was concerned, was that we, the fruit of her loins, learn to ride a horse. Horses, for Betty, had enormous socio-economic importance. Without a smattering of equestrian skills, my sister and I, according to Betty, were completely and utterly doomed to lives of mind-curdling mediocrity and misery.

'When you grow up and get a great job and your boss invites you to stay at his country house,' said Betty, as she envisaged our *Country Life* future, 'you will look like a right idiot if you can't stay on a bloody horse.'

In Betty's mind, horse riding opened up a Technicolor panorama of possibilities: it was the gateway to that fabulous world where square-jawed men in tweed sports coats and turtlenecks tossed Julie Christie-type girls in mini-kilts and Arran-knit sweaters into their Aston Martins and roared off to Elizabethan country houses for classy weekends of nouveau Beaujolais and fine dining.

I can't help feeling that Betty Life-Is-for-Living

Doonan, with her magazine subscriptions, her focus on life-enhancing pleasures, and her obsession with everything that was glamorous and international, was largely responsible for my fixation on the Beautiful People. Having never met any BPs, she had no idea that they were humour-impaired.

Every Saturday come rain or shine, Betty gave my sister and me half a crown each and sent us off, not to a country house, but to muddy Stokes' Farm, which was located in an area known as Bugs Bottom.

Here we mounted one of several ageing ponies and set off for an hour-long ride, ambling along country lanes without any specific goals, other than to *not* fall off. Every week it was the same. There was no fancy dressage or ribbon-strewn gymkhanas. Once in a while Mrs Stokes would drag some logs into the middle of a field, and we would jump over them. The rest of the time we trotted contentedly down the moist country lanes of Bugs Bottom. It was all very pleasant. In the fields on either side of us were cows belonging to Stokes and other farmers. They ate buttercups and batted their lashes at us.

On the occasion of the great penetration, the weather was particularly gorgeous. I was riding Jenny, a delicate, nervous pony, and my sister was riding Bess, a giant, grey, dappled carthorse.

It was fast approaching teatime. We were returning to the stable. Bess's shiny rump was undulating in front of me. I was fantasising about all the fabulous country weekends in my future. I was undecided about which role I would play. I could not choose between the Julie Christie part and a character of my own invention: the strangely-devoted-best-friend-of-the-square-jawed-male-lead.

A cuckoo called out from the copse of oak trees on the hill. Bees collected honey from the clover on either side of the path. It was an almost sickeningly beautiful English summer afternoon.

Suddenly the bucolic serenity was shattered by the thundering of hooves. A charging colt came hurtling towards the fence and skidded to a halt, sending my Jenny into a twitter of nervous tap dancing.

His eyes were wild with unbridled passion. He snorted maniacally and began to run backwards and forwards along the fence. Large gobs of snow-white foam fell from his quivering lips. He had just found the woman of his dreams. I tightened my thighs around my mount and assessed the situation: as long as he stayed on the other side of the fence, we – Jenny and I – had nothing to worry about.

Then I noticed *it*.

There was something strange and alien dangling between his legs. Clamped to this poor animal's genitals was what appeared to be a large red vacuum cleaner attachment. The object in question looked exactly like the crevice nozzle from Betty's new Hoover. No wonder he was galloping in such a panic: he wanted somebody to remove this red, rubbery, hideous, tubelike thing from around his willie.

Then with a shudder, I realised the ghastly truth. That's no vacuum cleaner attachment! That *is* his penis!

Suddenly, everything went into car-crash mode.

Incensed with erotic arousal, the colt flew over the fence. His crevice nozzle cleared the barbed wire by millimetres.

Within a matter of seconds, he had jumped onto poor Jenny's back. Horror of horrors: his grassy, passionate breath was hitting the back of my neck, filling my nostrils and uncurling my hair. More disturbingly and unforgettably, there was *a hoof on either side of me*!

This animal was attempting to skewer *us* with his crevice nozzle!

Jenny reared and bolted. Weeping and shrieking, I hung on. The colt fell off, only to stumble and reattach himself, plonking those shiny young hooves on either side of me and butting my back with his snorting muzzle.

I whacked him round the head with my riding crop.

He seemed not to notice me. He was blinded by lust.

While this ghastly violation of myself and Jenny lasted about a minute, I feel it is safe to say that its untold psychological impact lingers to this very day. I cannot even look at a vacuum cleaner without experiencing an odd sinking feeling followed by a flash of dread.

The colt then turned his attention to Bess and her high, majestic rump. He and his nozzle disengaged from me and Jenny, and charged ahead. He then tried repeatedly and unsuccessfully to climb onto my sister's stately mount. Bess wobbled and shook with righteous indignation. She slapped him round the face with her sumptuous tail and shot him a look of regal disdain, which said, 'Begone! You are less than the manure on my queenly hooves.'

The colt doubled back and refocused his efforts on the infinitely more conquerable Jenny. Before I knew it, I was bookended once more by those hateful hooves. Where was this going to end?

Then, salvation!

Mrs Stokes, hearing our screams of terror, came charging over a hillock. I fully anticipated that she might shoot the colt with the rifle which she kept on the mantelpiece in her office.

She was carrying a broom.

She was laughing.

She thought the whole thing was hilarious.

We dismounted and leapt on our muddy bicycles. We could not get out of Bugs Bottom fast enough.

That night, my sister and I were quite subdued. We lacked the vocabulary to describe the mayhem to which we had been subjected.

'If that is the kind of thing that happens during those fancy country weekends, then count me out,' said Shelagh as she wriggled out of her miniature jodhpurs.

'Well, I'm still going,' I said, as if our fancy country weekends had already been arranged and booked.

'And you're still going riding?' asked my sister, sound-ing mystified.

'Oh, no. I'm just going to tell the lady of the house that I've got a headache, then we'll stay behind together and arrange flowers and put on plays,' I replied as I scrubbed colt slobber off the back of my jacket.

Chapter 17

BLANCHE

Hᴇ ɪꜱ ᴀ twinkie* and I am a troll.
The year is 1994. I have a new boyfriend. It's a
May–December romance. I am 42, and he is 28.

The person in question is a clay-spattered potter called
Jonny. Though, like most twinkies, he is attractive and
funny, I find I have nagging reservations about Jonny: I'm
not sure about dating anyone who is so young that he is
not familiar with the names Claudine Longet and Ruth

---

*Twinkie: old-school Greenwich Village vernacular referring to a fresh-faced male
frequently seen in the company of less fresh-faced males, a.k.a. trolls.

Buzzi. I am worried this might be the beginning of a trend. Am I doomed to grow old dating progressively younger and younger chaps? Is this the beginning of my *Roman Spring*?

In contrast to me, Jonny does not seem even remotely disturbed by the age difference. On the contrary. He takes great delight in revisiting the issue over and over again in an ever more baroque and sarcastic fashion.

'Have you been back to Pompeii since . . . you know . . . *it*? Hard to talk about it, is it? I understand. Maybe we could go next summer. I've never been, and it would probably provide you with some sense of . . . closure.'

'By the way, how was the Renaissance? Was it really as great as they say it was?'

Verbal retaliation on my part is a complete waste of time. It is virtually impossible, in our youth-obsessed culture, to mock somebody for being young.

'You . . . you . . . *toddler,* you!'

'Why, you're nothing more than a cheap little zygote!'

There is no such thing as a *young* fart.

The only thing I can come up with by way of reprisal is to mock Jonny's crunchy granola profession. 'Where are your Jesus sandals? I can't believe I'm dating a potter! Sheesh!'

'Correction: a gerontophile potter.'

Under this welter of witty badinage, I have no choice other than to admit defeat. Jonny, or *my* Jonny, as I like to call him, wins hands down. He is young and I am old.

Before I began dating my Jonny, it never occurred to me that I, myself, me, was anything other than incredibly young. Young. Young. Young. Thanks to Jonny, I must now face the fact that I am a middle-aged person.

Prompted by this realisation, I take a long, hard look in the mirror. Jonny is correct: I am no longer in the first flush of youth. Yes, I have hair. Yes, I have teeth. But there are crow's feet and there are age spots. I have not yet become jowly and hideous, but my prettiest years are definitely behind me. Old age, though still just a distant will-o'-the-wisp, is now, thanks to my Jonny, lurking on the horizon. Though still able to skip at a fair clip, I now wear reading glasses and feel the cold horribly: a significant part of my waking hours is spent with a cardigan draped ridiculously over my shoulders.

And another thing: horror of horrors, I am no longer able to eat in a tidy fashion. I have become that thing my mother always warned me about. I have become a *messy eater*. This is a phenomenon that Betty always highlighted as being the grimmest and most unattractive consequence of advancing age.

'It happens to everyone. The minute you hit middle age – bang! – you become a *messy eater*.'

There's a morsel of food stuck to the middle of my Prada trouser fly. Saffron rice. We ate Indian two nights ago. It's been stuck there for two days. I feel a pang of melancholy. In these congealed grains, I can clearly see my slobbering dotage. When Jonny is 50, I will be 64.

Thwap!

My Jonny slaps me on the bum, yanking me from my reverie. He kisses me goodbye and Rollerblades off to his clay commune.

So what if I'm 42! Life is great! We are happy!

A 14-year age difference is nothing as long as you are with the right person and you have the right attitude! May–December romances are not such a big deal: animals have them all the time, and so do celebs! Liz Taylor and Larry Fortensky! Anna Nicole Smith and whatever that guy's name was. Krystle and Blake Carrington!

Like the Carringtons, Jonny and I adore each other, and that's what counts.

I run to the window and drop a pair of his underwear four floors onto his departing head. He shakes his fist at me.

'I may not be young, but I'm definitely *young at heart*!' I yell and let forth a peal of theatrical laughter.

Two months later. Thanksgiving. It's time to meet the folks. Panic.

Everything I have heard about Jonny's family makes me slightly uneasy: they sound so alarmingly respectable. There are no loonies or lobotomies. Despite his bohemian trade, my Jonny is, or so it seems, just a nice upper-middle-class Jewish boy from a New Jersey farm town. His grandfathers were not hard-drinking bon viveurs, they were judges, both of them. These pillars of the community devoted their lives to reprimanding and sentencing the likes of me during my plaid-bondage years. Among all this upstanding citizenry, I can find only one tiny soupçon of scandal or intrigue: Jonny's paternal nana and zadie were first cousins.

On this unsullied landscape, Jonny's recent disclosure about his sexual orientation looms quite large. Though generally supportive, the Adler family are, according to Jonny, still 'coming to terms' with the fact that he is gay. Inbreeding = no problem. Gay = oy veh!

A new challenge is about to test their mettle, in the shape of moi. They are about to confront the reality that their youngest son not only is a friend of Dorothy's but has fallen madly in love with a known homosexual *d'un certain age*.

My panic about the Jersey trip increases. I am convinced that, at the very least, I will get arrested for trying to cross state lines with a twinkie.

What to do?

There is no time for a rejuvenating face lift, or even a skin peel. I could tape up my face, but that would involve keeping a hat, or a wig, on all weekend.

Botox? In 1994 it was still being tested on gerbils. Maybe I could go to the Botox headquarters and tell the researchers that I am a gerbil and get me some.

Make-up? I want Jonny's family to think Clint Eastwood, not Gary Glitter.

I take the only possible course of action open to me: backlighting! I decide to accept Jonny's invitation but to remain softly lit for the entire weekend. This will obviously present myriad challenges, but hey, it worked for Blanche DuBois in *A Streetcar Named Desire*, and it would work for me.

Blanche deluded everyone about her age and her past by lurking in the shadows and refusing to go out until it was dark. It worked like a dream. Everything would have been fine if that nasty, common Mitch (Karl Malden) had not come along.

Mitch: I've never had a real good look at you, Blanche. Let's turn the light on here. (*He tears the paper lantern off the lightbulb. She utters a frightened gasp.*)

If it hadn't been for that prying Mitch, Mademoiselle DuBois would probably have made it all the way to the insane asylum without anyone guessing her age.

One chilly Friday night in late 1994, Jonny and I barrel into the Holland Tunnel. Maybe *barrel* is not quite the word. I have always been a bit of a slow driver. Once I was pulled over by a cop on the Hollywood Freeway and given a ticket for going 30 miles per hour. I was enjoying the view, what can I tell you?

While I drive, my Jonny tells me bloodcurdling stories about our destination, the southern New Jersey farm town of Bridgeton. His description makes Reading, my lacklustre birthplace, seem like Monte Carlo. The Beautiful People have certainly never been to Bridgeton. The only Bridgetonian celebrity Jonny can cite is a flamboyant black cross-dresser, nicknamed Charlie Powderpuff. Charlie made headlines in the local paper after being beaten to death with two-by-fours in an alley.

Welcome to the lovely Garden State!

We pull up in front of a groovy modern home, circa 1968. My geriatric driving has served me well. Night has fallen. One point for Blanche!

Inside, Jonny's family – parents Cynthia and Harry, and brother and sister David and Amy – are waiting in the ultramod family room. I dash into the fray and position myself in front of the TV. Confidently backlit by its powerful rays, I brace myself for introductions.

The greetings are warm, effusive, but brief. Everybody is preoccupied. It is clear that they had been awaiting our arrival with a certain amount of impatience.

Suddenly there is a mad dash to the kitchen, where many cruel, unforgiving fluorescent lights blaze. I peer cautiously round the corner. The entire family, including Jonny, is clustered around the kitchen table like a pack of dogs. They are shrieking at the tops of their lungs, and they appear to be feeding.

Every now and then a family member comes up for air. I see to my horror that they were all masticating large, pinky-red, pungent boiled crabs.

The spectre of inbreeding looms over the repast.

'Blue crabs,' yells Jonny in an outdoor voice between mouthfuls of foul-smelling crabmeat. 'It's a South Jersey thing.'

I wonder if the shouting is a result of inbreeding, or is it, like the blue crabs, simply 'a South Jersey thing'. And then I remember that Harry, Jonny's dad, is deaf.

I'm starting to relax. Snarky, hilarious, warm, and welcoming, the Adlers have the makings of ideal in-laws. As an added bonus Amy, and Jonny's mom Cynthia, are vain and attractive. Blanche is beginning to feel quite at home.

Then everything goes all nasty.

The crab course is followed by a local delicacy: an enormous platter of deep-fried mishigas.*

The subject of sleeping arrangements has come up. Harry jump-starts the mishigas by suggesting that I might like to sleep on the couch in the den.

I can see his point. My Jonny's bed is quite narrow, and, at the end of the day, my Jonny is also his Jonny, and he is protective of his Jonny. Harry is not about to relinquish his Jonny to the backlit, middle-aged stranger in the faux chinchilla sweater.

Jonny gets irate. He takes offence that I might not be permitted to sleep with him. Amy and David get to sleep with their boyfriends and girlfriends, etc. This is discrimination!

Feeling like the world's biggest pervert, I shrivel further into the shadows. By this point I am identifying

---

*Mishigas: Yiddish, crazy Jewish in-laws expressing themselves in an uninhibited fashion.

more with John Wayne Gacy than with Blanche DuBois. I scamper upstairs and hide in the bathroom.

Breathe!

I compose myself by taking an inventory of Cynthia's cosmetics. This proves to be a moderately effective mishigas antidote. As I contemplate her various applicators, I wonder how many sables have to die to make one of her oversized blusher brushes. Look at all these eye shadows! How often does she recolour her lids? Is blue eye shadow over, or so totally over that it's just totally *back*? Ah, mascara! I've always been jealous that women got to wear mascara and men didn't. Who wouldn't want to wear a product called Ultra-Lash? And look how the packaging has changed over the years! It seems like only yesterday that Betty and her contemporaries were spitting into those adorable little cakes of black pigment and then attempting to apply it to their lashes with those horrid, clogged, little mini-toothbrushes.

Gradually, the cringing mishigas subsides. I find that I am left with a vague feeling of amusement and familiarity. I like my new in-laws. I begin to suspect, with growing relief, that Jonny's family might be just as insane as mine, if not more so.

I open the bathroom door and creep down the corridor towards Jonny's room. Suddenly I hear a 'psst!' It is Jonny's sister, Amy. She beckons me towards her room.

'I want to show you my new dress,' she says breathily, sounding like, and resembling, Anne, the 'Gillian Girl' from *Valley of the Dolls*.

Perching on the corner of her bed, I relax and survey the scene. Though Amy is in her 30s and holding down a gruelling and very grown-up job at a fancy New York law firm, her childhood bedroom still has an eerie, doll-strewn, prepubescent quality. It is about to get a lot more eerie.

With a ceremonial air, Miss Adler opens the doors to her closet.

She pulls out a nifty Dolce & Gabbana cocktail dress, the kind of thing Sophia Loren might have worn in one of her streets-of-Naples 1960s movies. I give it the thumbs up, and we bond over our mutual love of a good frock.

I am just about to rejoin the mishigas festival down-stairs when I notice a series of rectangular boxes nestling on the top shelf of her closet. These boxes are larger than a shirt box but smaller than an old-fashioned gown box. Intrigued, I ask about the contents. Amy smiles enthusiastically and grabs the nearest box. After much untying of ribbons and uncrunching of ancient tissue paper, she proudly holds up a dress. It is a tiny, summery Shirley Temple number with embroidered yellow flowers and a very full skirt. It's about twice the size of an oven mitt.

'I wore it to kindergarten with matching yellow stock-ings. Every day I would twirl around and show the boys my underwear. I had many admirers.'

I am speechless. Being of diminutive stature, I am quite tempted to try it on myself.

Encouraged by my enthusiasm, Amy unfurls another frock and then another. Together we take a wistfully fascinating tour of her elaborate and meticulously maintained childhood wardrobe. Box after box is opened and then lovingly closed again. There are special occasion dresses in dark satins and pastel organdies. Day dresses are plaid or tweed or cotton gingham for summer.

As she shows me each frock, Amy recounts the occasion upon which it was worn, the picnics, the bar mitzvahs, the weddings and birthdays. It is a sentimental trip down memory lane, and one which seems to give Amy herself a surreal amount of dreamy pleasure.

I am feeling quite jealous, and just a tad resentful.

No wonder I can't remember anything pleasant: I didn't have the right frocks!

Whereas I can remember only the jarring occurrences – the flashers, the dentures, the pustules, the tarts and the embarrassments – Amy seems joyously and effortlessly focused on all the magical Hallmark moments. None of the events she describes is particularly memorable. However, with the aid of her frocks, she has found a way to reconnect with the joy of each occasion.

'What a fabulous childhood you must have had,' I remark as I admire the faggoting on a purple linen number.

'Yes, it was perfect,' replied Amy, 'utterly, utterly perfect.'

Jonny interrupts our tête-à-tête. He has resolved the issue of sleeping quarters and instructs me to follow him.

I skip down the hall towards his bedroom feeling totally at home. My new sister-in-law is not only gorgeous but completely cuckoo. In fact, Jonny's entire family are every bit as deranged as mine, only they live in New Jersey, are slightly inbred, and have Marimekko shades on every window. We have far more in common than I would have ever imagined. Though I have successfully managed to stay backlit for the entire evening, I am beginning to suspect that I might be wasting my time.

Jonny's bedroom, like Amy's, is frozen in time. It looks as if nothing has been moved since junior high school. Every surface seems to be covered in toy cars and Snoopys. I decide to go to sleep quickly, before I start to feel creepy and pervy again.

The next morning gets off to a good start. Over breakfast, I bond with Jonny's brother, David, who has devoted a substantial amount of his late 20s and early 30s to researching the eating habits of the late, great Elvis Presley. He has befriended the cooks who fried squirrels for Elvis and the loving housekeepers who unwittingly clogged the Presley bowels and arteries with fried peanut-butter-and-banana sandwiches. Magnanimously, he agrees to share some of the recipes with me. I leap up to grab a pen and run smack dab into . . . Granny.

Jonny had previously warned me about the charismatic and combative Granny. She (aged 90) and Jonny's mum, Cynthia (aged 60), were recently asked to leave Saks Fifth Avenue after a mother-and-daughter shopping trip disintegrated into a nuclear explosion of mishigas.

Granny had not been part of the previous evening's crab-munching reception. Having retired to her bed early, she was now fighting fit and ready for some action.

Granny fixes her unwavering gaze on me.

The house is so white and mod and stark, there is nowhere for me to hide.

Granny corners me in front of the toaster oven.

I am struck by her appearance. For a woman her age, she is exceptionally chic, impeccably accessorised and amazingly well-coiffed. Or at least her wig is well-coiffed.

We stare into each other's eyes.

The New Jersey sunlight pours in and illuminates our stand-off, our respective outfits and our ages.

I feel as if I'm in a movie.

I am Blanche.

Granny is playing the part of Mitch.

Maybe Granny originated the role of Mitch.

Her piercing gaze deconstructs my ensemble. Is that a look of disgust or envy? I can't really tell. Maybe she has never seen a man wearing faux chinchilla. She seems displeased. Maybe Granny is a fur activist. Her eye is drawn to the ring that adorns my pinkie. It glints. Finally she focuses on the large fur hat which I have elected to wear indoors because it is, in fact, quite chilly.

Granny puts two and two together and comes up with Charlie Powderpuff.

Granny retreats to her room.

I lean nonchalantly on the toaster oven and attempt to conceal my cringing panic by exuding an aura of international savoir faire.

I half expect her to return to the kitchen swinging a two-by-four.

Granny remains in her room. Granny weeps audibly.

Sparks fly out of the mishigas metre. It is smoking.

'Meeting new people is really wonderful,' I muse as I toast myself a crumpet. 'New friends can have a transformative effect on one's life. Why, when I met Jonny, I found out that I was middle aged. And now, whaddya know, Granny meets me and she finds out that Jonny is a fagele.'

Granny emerges from her room some time after lunch, at which point I decide to go on the offensive.

'What a fabulous suit you are wearing!' I exclaim, referring to the cobalt blue St John knit with the gleaming gold buttons.

'Black people love my clothing,' says Granny, caressing a large Chanel earring and shifting from one Ferragamo heel to the other. 'They love colour. I love colour. The women in my building don't appreciate it. They are boring. I have nothing in common with them. You see [beat], I was married to a judge.'

Granny's deadpan declamatory delivery is not only hilarious but also highly informative. All has been revealed. Combining what Jonny has told me with what I have just heard, I now understand who Granny is.

Granny came to America nearly a hundred years ago. She bought nice clothes. She aspired up, not down. She discovered the power of accessories. Out of all the people in the house, Granny and I have the most in common. She is a superannuated female version of me, a feisty first-generation immigrant who enjoys dressing up and has clawed her way to the middle without really knowing why.

Granny and I bond, effortlessly.

'Can I see your bracelet?' I ask, after my eye is drawn to the rope of gold on her right wrist.

'Tiffany's. It's my Roy Cohn bracelet. My husband bought it for me after he won a big case against Cohn.'

After discussing all her jewellery, we embark on an enthusiastic rant about how generally more fabulous we are than anyone else in the Western Hemisphere. We are now a 'we'. Everything is about how incredibly great and special we are and how pedestrian/uninteresting/unstylish the rest of humanity is.

We get quite carried away with ourselves. We become quite obnoxious, Granny and I. And why not?

We are the Beautiful People, and we know it.

~

Jonny and I drive Granny back to Philadelphia.

After being in the car for about 20 minutes, Granny and I begin to calm down. We have finally run out of self-congratulatory steam. Granny becomes a little contemplative. She takes a long look at me and my Jonny. The realisation that we are a happy couple is starting to sink in.

'I always thought that when I reached old age I would sit in a rocking chair and stare into the middle distance like Whistler's mother . . .' She pauses and touches the side of her wig with a cupped hand. 'But you know what? Nothing changes. The mishigas just keeps on coming.'

We take Granny up to her chicly decorated apartment. In the hallways we meet some of her co-residents.

None of them are as fab as Granny.

POSTSCRIPT

THE FLOOR PILLOW

In 1977, the year of the Queen's silver jubilee, an over-weight punk-rock friend pogoed onto the floor pillow, causing it to explode and fill our home with crumbling Styrofoam nuggets. Biddie and I dragged the half-empty sack out to the nearest bus stop and left it waiting poignantly in the rain.

In what can only be described as a coincidence of gargantuan proportions, Jonathan Adler, my Jonny, the love of my life, now designs and manufactures, along with his ceramics, gorgeous squishy floor pillows. Maybe I'm biased, but his floor pillows seem so much nicer than the one Biddie and I dragged around London for so many years.

JAMES BIDDLECOMBE

I'm happy to report that the incredible and talented Biddie has outlived the floor pillow. He continues to

perform, delighting audiences from Stepney to Ibiza. He
even has his own website – www.biddie.co.uk. As I write
he is illuminating the pantomime season at the Malvern
Festival Theatre and wowing the audience with his inter-
pretation of a character called Widow Twanky in *Aladdin*.
'She's a very lanky Twanky who doesn't hold with hanky
panky!!' Despite our advancing years, we continue to call
each other 'daughter!' He continues to insult me about
my lack of height. He recently sent me a bogus circus-
midget application form with a sequin glued to the
outside of the envelope. I was quite taken in. I should
have smelled a rat when I got to the bit where I was asked
to specify my 'height (above sawdust)'.

TERRY DOONAN

My dad outlived Betty by seven years. He missed her
horribly and assuaged his pain by prominently displaying
a pair of her high-heeled lace-up ankle boots on his
mantelpiece to remind him of the good times.

SHELAGH DOONAN

My gay sister remains happily married to a lady called
Anna, who is a leading light in the South London belly-
dancing community. They have a gorgeous daughter
called Tanya, who is much smarter and taller than I was at
her age.

Upon reading the 'Gifts' chapter, Shelagh wrote to me with her reactions. Here is an excerpt from her letter:

How did we both turn out queer? Who knows! Like you, I was simply trying to make sense of who I was. Loved everything you wrote with the notable exception of your depiction of me in the 1980s: it was an incredible time of personal and political ferment: nuclear weapons, exhausting experiments in non-monogamy, excitement and subversiveness in discos with names like *Daisies* and *Rackets!* It was all very different from the Slag/Shelagh who emerges in your pages – earnest, grumpy and a bit dowdy, like the dykes who (rarely) appear in *Will & Grace*.

                              Your loving sister XXX

In her letter she also accuses me of deliberately characterising lesbians as stylistically challenged, bum-bag-toting drears in order to create a foil for my own spotlight-grabbing persona.

Naturally, there is not one iota of truth in these outrageous and totally unfounded accusations. I am chalking her feelings up to gay sibling rivalry.

My very first decorative accessory

In 2000 I was clearing out my parents' attic when I stumbled upon my first great love, that red glass decanter.

I dragged it back to New York, where it sits proudly on my desk, a testament to my congenital affinity for camp and exotica.

My fellow college vermin

Joy stopped drinking astringent and had three kids. Sadly, Rose died in 2001, leaving a gorgeous daughter called Eleanor, who so far shows no signs of wanting to make cottage cheese in her tights.

Uncle Ken

Though fraught with problems, Ken's marriage to Pat endured. They remained together for the rest of his tormented and difficult life, proving the old adage that there is indeed *someone for everyone*.

Ken has long since departed for that great floor pillow in the sky, where I hope God has seen fit to restore his sanity. I would like to think that he now spends his days lounging about, rolling his own cigarettes, and discussing my inclination to write confessional books with Terry, Betty and blind Aunt Phyllis, Lassie and a happily unschizophrenic Narg.

The Malaysian Simulator

Long gone, as is the Commonwealth Institute itself. Probably shut down by the health authorities, which is just as well. It was a breeding ground for cold germs. Biddie caught an atrocious flu after nodding off and snoozing through half a dozen presentation cycles.

My sanity

Haven't lost it yet. There's still plenty of time. Head thrashing recurs once in a while. My dog, Liberace, usually wakes me up by licking my face.

Skipping

Still a firm believer. I don't recommend doing it in public, unless you are either very old or very young.

The Colostomy Bags

I drove them around for a few more years. Never did find a use for them. I hope I never will.

Rita

I have no idea what happened to Rita, the tart.

I try to conjure happy endings for my long-lost neighbour. Maybe she found God or won the lottery and bought a pub on the Costa Brava, where, tanned and podgy, she now entertains retired members of the off-track betting community.

Somehow I doubt it. Rita's willingness to embrace her role as underclass slag did not bode well for her future. She was a perfectly styled victim who might just as well have had a sign on her back which read, 'Please don't invite me for a weekend at your Elizabethan country house. Instead, please bludgeon me to death with a large wrench and throw me in an alley.' No amount of floor pillows could get her out of the gutter and into one of Nigella Lawson's dinner parties.

The misery of her life reaches across the decades and yanks at my heart strings.

Why do I care? Having myself travelled the bumpy road from *common* to *vaguely presentable*, I wish only the best for others.

THE BEAUTIFUL PEOPLE

Quelle surprise! They were right under my nose all the time.

Wait! I feel another *Wizard of Oz* moment coming on:

> *if I ever go looking for my heart's desire again*
> *I won't look any further than my own backyard.*

No wonder Dorothy has so many friends.

We're British Innit

THE REAL CITIZENSHIP TEST

From Alcopops to *X Factor* via Churchill and Ovaltine, Iain Aitch celebrates modern-day Britain in this acutely observed and hilariously funny A–Z of all that we are and all that we do.

Whether it's our insatiable passion for tea, a sense of fair play, our desire to form an orderly queue at the drop of a hat, or simply our ability to rattle on endlessly about the weather, everything you've ever regarded as being uniquely British is within these pages. Unlike the Government's Citizenship Test, this is the real Britain – the little land that we affectionately know and love for all its quirks and traditions.

Guaranteed to bring a smile of recognition to even the stiffest of upper lips.

ISBN 978-0-00-727132-0

To order this title please call our Customer Hotline number.

Tel: 0870 787 1724 • Fax: 0870 787 1725

CREDIT CARDS ACCEPTED

For further information about other books from Collins please visit

www.collins.co.uk

Getting Into Guinness

ONE MAN'S LONGEST, FASTEST, HIGHEST JOURNEY INSIDE THE WORLD'S MOST FAMOUS RECORD BOOK

A quirky history of the many madcap attempts to get into *The Guinness Book Of Records* told by a man determined to set his own world record.

When Larry Olmstead decided to get into *Guinness* by setting a new world record, he began to wonder about all those people who had gone before him.

Now, for the first time, Larry Olmstead takes you behind the records to learn about the colourful characters who set them. Meet the Frenchman Michael Lotito who won the title of greatest omnivore for his ability to eat up to two pounds of metal a day (he's even eaten a supermarket trolley), or find out about the oldest vomit in the world, aged over 160 million years.

This is the hilarious true story of the quirkiest, most memorable records and one man's attempts to join them by setting his very own world record.

ISBN 978-0-00-726129-1

Coming soon to a bookshop near you in September 2008

To order this title please call our Customer Hotline number.

Tel: 0870 787 1724 • Fax: 0870 787 1725

CREDIT CARDS ACCEPTED

For further information about other books from Collins please visit

www.collins.co.uk

Daily Candy A to Z
AN INSIDER'S GUIDE TO THE SWEET LIFE

You have questions. *Daily Candy A to Z* has answers.

From the writers of the favourite free daily email for hundreds of thousands of women around the globe about fashion, food and culture, *Daily Candy* has finally entered the real world with this book of musings on style, love, work, shopping, and all the fundamentals you need to land yourself one sweet life.

This book will surprise, delight, and instruct its way into your stylish little heart. From how to pinch pennies, to how to splurge shamelessly, from doing unto others to doing your ex-boyfriend, *Daily Candy A to Z* is a book that's sure to bring a bit of relief to those lamenting the state of the world today.

You'll laugh (hopefully). You'll cry (OK, probably not). But your life will definitely be sweeter because of it.

ISBN 978-0-00-724254-2

To order this title please call our Customer Hotline number.

Tel: 0870 787 1724   •   Fax: 0870 787 1725

CREDIT CARDS ACCEPTED

For further information about other books from Collins please visit

www.collins.co.uk